10/13/64

# SOME BRITISH
# COLLECTORS OF MUSIC
## c. 1600 – 1960

# SOME BRITISH COLLECTORS OF MUSIC

## c. 1600 – 1960

BY

A. HYATT KING

*Sandars Reader in Bibliography, and*
*Sometime Scholar of King's College, Cambridge*

CAMBRIDGE

AT THE UNIVERSITY PRESS

1963

PUBLISHED BY

THE SYNDICS OF THE CAMBRIDGE UNIVERSITY PRESS

Bentley House, 200 Euston Road, London, N.W. 1

American Branch: 32 East 57th Street, New York 22, N.Y.

West African Office: P.O. Box 33, Ibadan, Nigeria

©

CAMBRIDGE UNIVERSITY PRESS

1963

*Printed in Great Britain at the University Printing House, Cambridge*
*(Brooke Crutchley, University Printer)*

*To*
C. B. OLDMAN

# PREFACE

The text of this book consists of the lectures which I delivered at Cambridge during Michaelmas Term 1961 as Sandars Reader in Bibliography. The original typescript has been read by Mr Charles Cudworth, Professor Thurston Dart, Mr O. W. Neighbour, Dr C. B. Oldman, C.B., C.V.O., Mr John Pashby and Miss Pamela Willetts. They have given me many useful additions and corrections which I have incorporated into the version printed here and I am deeply grateful to them.

But even with this improvement and such supplementary information as I have added myself, these pages can only offer an introduction to one aspect of a very large and strangely neglected subject. Although the literature about the history of book-collecting is extensive and of respectable antiquity, very little has ever been written on those who have collected music in any part of the world. Some indication of the possible extent of this topic is to be found in a valuable paper which the Comtesse de Chambure wrote in 1959, 'Les Collections privées de livres et d'instruments de musique d'autrefois et d'aujourd'hui'.[1] Strong evidence of the close link between the collecting of music and the collecting of instruments is also found in the fact that, as sale-catalogues show, many generations of British collectors have regarded the one as an essential complement to the other. This is another neglected subject which would certainly repay investigation.

In the course of the lectures, I said something about the transmission and location of manuscripts and rare or unique printed items. Here, too, is a new wide field for future study, for which there are few sources ready to

---

[1] See *Music, Libraries and Instruments*, ed. Unity Sherrington and Guy Oldham (London, 1961), pp. 131–47. (*Proceedings of the Joint Congress of the International Association of Music Libraries and the Galpin Society*, held at Cambridge in 1959.)

hand. The admirable indexes to Augustus Hughes-Hughes's three-volume *Catalogue of Manuscript Music in the British Museum* (1906–9) name owners meticulously.  So does the index to the typewritten *Catalogue of the Manuscripts in the Library of the Royal College of Music* (1931), compiled by Barclay Squire.  But for manuscripts in other libraries and for the rarities of printed music there are no methodical indexes to ownership at all.  A certain number of ownerships are mentioned incidentally in the entries of a few printed catalogues such as those of the music in Christ Church, St Michael's College, Tenbury and the Fitzwilliam Museum.  The Bodleian's *Summary Catalogue of Western Manuscripts* gives many names of owners in the descriptions, but few, alas, in the index.  Much of the evidence would therefore still have to be brought together from signatures on fly-leaves and title-pages, and from bookplates and labels on bindings.  However laborious this task, it would in time add enormously to our knowledge of past collectors of music.

Music, like books, has attracted collectors in every imaginable walk of British life, from the professional classes to the highest in the land. The evidence for royalty as collectors of music is largely to be found in the Royal Music Library, about which I published two articles in *The Book Collector* some time before my election as Sandars Reader.  As it was impracticable to work these articles into the text of my lectures, I have reprinted them here, in a revised form.  For kind permission to do so, my thanks are due to Mr John Hayward, C.B.E., editorial director of *The Book Collector*.  Here I would also express my gratitude to Mr R. C. Mackworth-Young, M.V.O., Librarian to H.M. the Queen, for the information which he generously gave me from the Royal Archives at Windsor Castle, and to which he has added since the articles were first printed.

In order to make the book of some use as a work of reference, I have added lists of collectors which include the names of many others besides those mentioned in the text of the lectures. Not all, perhaps, are collectors within the terms of the definition which I have attempted in my first lecture, but none is entirely devoid of historical or bibliographical interest. It will be seen that for a score or so of early collectors I have been unable to find any copy of the catalogue of a sale, although the sale certainly took place and the catalogue was published. If any of these are to be found in libraries or elsewhere, I should be very glad to be informed.

The time at my disposal, both for the writing of the lectures and the revision of them for publication, was unfortunately limited. Most of my research was centred on the British Museum with its unique collection of sale-catalogues, but I was well aware that much important information must lie elsewhere. To my regret, I could not visit all the extant collections which I have mentioned and study them in detail. A score or so in London, Oxford and Cambridge I did visit, with the kind help of the librarians concerned. Otherwise, I have had to rely on such catalogues or descriptions as were available in print or typescript and on correspondence.

For details of collections now in libraries scattered throughout Britain and elsewhere and for numerous facts about collectors of many generations I have to thank librarians, scholars and members of the antiquarian-music trade. Either in answer to my inquiries, or voluntarily, having heard of my work, they have contributed valuable information, much of which is new.

I would therefore express my gratitude to: Miss Jean Allan, Librarian of the Reid Music Library, Edinburgh; Miss Barbara Banner, Librarian of the Royal College of Music, London; Mr Hermann Baron; Mr Philip Brett; Mr Charles Cudworth, Librarian of the Pendlebury Library, Cambridge; Miss Margaret Deneke; Mr Heinrich Eisemann; Mr Ifan Kyrle Fletcher; Miss Phyllis Giles, Librarian of the Fitzwilliam Museum, Cambridge; Mr R. Alec Harman, Lecturer in Music, Durham Colleges in the University of Durham; Dr R. J. Hayes, Librarian of the National Library of Ireland, Dublin; Mr W. G. Hiscock, Deputy Librarian, Christ Church, Oxford;

Mr Cecil Hopkinson; Dr R. W. Hunt, Keeper of Western Manuscripts, Bodleian Library, Oxford; Mr F. J. E. Hurst, Deputy Librarian, Trinity College Library, Dublin; Mr F. G. B. Hutchings, City Librarian, Leeds Public Libraries; Mr R. W. Ketton-Cremer; Dr R. W. Ladborough, Fellow and Pepysian Librarian, Magdalene College, Cambridge; Mrs Valerie Leach, Librarian of the Faculty of Music, University of Oxford; Dr Peter Le Huray, Fellow of St Catharine's College, Cambridge; Miss Marion Linton, Assistant Keeper in charge of the Music Room, National Library of Scotland, Edinburgh; Mr Hugh McClean; Mr Philip L. Miller, Chief of the Music Division, New York Public Library; Dr A. N. L. Munby, Fellow and Librarian, King's College, Cambridge; Mr Percy Muir; Mrs Ruth Noyes, Librarian, Cecil Sharp House, London; Mr J. C. T. Oates, Under-Librarian, University Library, Cambridge; Mr Peter Pagan, Director, Victoria Art Gallery and Municipal Libraries, Bath; Miss Joan Pemberton, Librarian, Central Music Library, London; Mr H. L. Pink, Under-Librarian, University Library, Cambridge; Mr Albi Rosenthal; Mr Harold Watkins Shaw, Hon. Librarian of St Michael's College, Tenbury; Mr Alexander Small, Chief Librarian of Dundee Public Libraries; Dr John Stevens, Fellow of Magdalene College, Cambridge; Mr Walter Stock, Librarian of the Royal Academy of Music, London; Mr J. E. Thomas, City Librarian, Cardiff Public Libraries; Mrs A. P. Vlasto, Librarian of the Rowe Music Library, King's College, Cambridge; Professor Sir Jack Westrup, Heather Professor of Music, University of Oxford; Dr J. A. Woods, Lecturer in American History, School of History, Leeds University.

A number of collectors of the present day have been so good as to let me have information about their possessions and to permit me to publish it in this book. My cordial thanks are due to: Mr Christopher Finzi; Mr Walter N. H. Harding; Mr Arthur Hedley; Mr J. E. Kite; Mr Vere Pilkington; Mr Raymond Russell; Mr Ronald Stevenson; Mr Alan Tyson; and the heirs of Stefan Zweig.

## Preface

I am very grateful to Mr H. M. Nixon for most of the information which I have given about the dates of various bindings.

To my wife I owe much for her skill in typing the final version of the text of the lectures and the appendixes.

My last—but by no means least—debt of gratitude is to the Syndics of the Cambridge University Press for having undertaken the publication of the book, and to members of their staff for the care they have lavished on its production.

A. H. K.

LONDON
*December 1962*

# CONTENTS

# LIST OF PLATES

*The plates are bound in between pp. 64 and 65.*

# List of Plates

VIII A note of presentation to Joseph Warren in the autograph of Edward Francis Rimbault, followed by a note signed: J.M. (i.e. Julian Marshall), to explain the word 'late', presumably added by Warren (British Museum, Add. MS. 31550, fly-leaf).

## ACKNOWLEDGEMENTS

Plate I(*b*) is reproduced by permission of the Syndics of the Fitzwilliam Museum, Cambridge; pl. IV by permission of the Senior Registrar, Principal Probate Registry, Somerset House; the remainder by courtesy of the Trustees of the British Museum.

# LECTURE I

## INTRODUCTION: SOURCES AND PRINCIPLES. STUARTS AND GEORGIANS TO 1799

If one reads the typescript or printed texts of past Sandars lectures, one finds that there are, broadly speaking, two ways in which successive Readers have opened their first lecture. Some have plunged boldly into their subject with complete detachment. Others—the majority, I think—have gradually established a twofold tradition. First, they have usually referred, sometimes with genuine embarrassment, sometimes with mock diffidence, to those who have preceded them in their chosen field. Second, they have usually declared the relevance of their subject to the terms of the Sandars bequest.

I must confess that I am by nature and habit one who respects a tradition. But on this occasion I am perhaps also fortunate in not having the shadow of any eminent predecessor looking, as it were, over my shoulder: for this is the first time since the inauguration of the Readership in 1895 that the invitation has been extended to one whose particular interest lies in the field of music. I am therefore deeply conscious of the signal honour I have received by my election.

The terms of the Sandars bequest are encouragingly wide. They require that 'the lecture is to embrace the subject of bibliography, palaeography, typography, bookbinding, book illustration, the science of books and manuscripts, and the arts relating thereto', but, further, that—subject to the discretion of the electors—the lectures are to be 'based upon and illustrated by examples contained in the University or college libraries'. I can only regret that within my own University I have had to ask for exemption from the requirement of drawing my examples solely from Cambridge libraries. But you may find some compensation in the fact that, in sum of excellence, variety and numbers, the music-collectors whose treasures have enriched Cambridge are hardly rivalled elsewhere, even though priority of collecting must be ceded to another university.

I realise that the topic I have chosen cannot of itself lay claim to originality, although I believe that the way I propose to develop it has not been explored before. It was Barclay Squire, the pioneer in this as in so many other fields of musical bibliography, who first assembled information about a few private collectors of music in Great Britain. His knowledge was committed to print as part of the article on musical libraries in the first and second editions of Grove's *Dictionary of Music*; in the third and fourth editions it was expanded by C. B. Oldman, and in the fifth it was remoulded by Charles Cudworth on even more generous lines than before. My debt to this article will be obvious, and in general I do not propose to repeat the details of collections given in it. But I shall take the subject a good deal farther afield, and for this my inspiration is partly due to another article in Grove, compiled by Otto Erich Deutsch, and headed, somewhat curiously, 'Collections, private'.

This article has, I think, some link with Cambridge, for it originated in the association between Deutsch and Paul Hirsch, which dated from about 1940 onwards. At their almost daily meetings, either in the University Library, or at a certain café in Trinity Street, these two bibliographers covered an inexhaustible range of musical topics, such as editions, issues, states, plate-numbers, *passe-partout* titles, publishers' catalogues, and, of course, libraries and collectors. One of the reference books they used when discussing collectors was the *List of Catalogues of English Book Sales, 1676–1900, now in the British Museum* (London, 1915). Among those who shared in their discussions from time to time was D. R. Wakeling, then a First Assistant in Cambridge University Library, where he was in charge of the Music Room. Wakeling undertook the labour of reading right through the 447 pages of the *List*, and made an abstract in typescript of all entries relating to music. (Copies of this abstract are now in the British Museum, and in Cambridge University Library, from which Wakeling retired in 1950.) This invaluable piece of work served as the basis for Deutsch's article 'Collections, private', in which he carried the terminal date, from his own researches, up to 1950. Deutsch included a number of early sales of which no catalogue is now extant; he also listed some other collections, preserved more or less intact by bequest and other means. Here I must state the crucial question that posed itself when I was planning these lectures. Should I deal with only fifty or so of the great collectors, treating each at considerable length? Or should I mention many more—three or four times as many, perhaps—giving due attention to the famous, but for the lesser mentioning only their general character and a few items of outstanding interest?

I chose the latter course, because it would bring to light the maximum of new facts and information. As nothing, apart from a few very incomplete lists and summaries, has been written about music-collectors, this was the deciding factor. Given this decision (which I hope will commend itself to my readers), Wakeling's abstract proved as invaluable to me as it had been to Deutsch. It was the springboard, as it were, from which I plunged into the deep end of the Museum's collection of catalogues. This proved to be not quite such a big task as it might seem, for statistical reasons.

Wakeling's total is 337, of which 213 are auctions of music and musical literature assembled by men—and a few women—named on the title-pages of the catalogues. There are, besides, thirty-one collections described as the property of 'a collector', 'an amateur', 'a distinguished professor' and the like. (Twenty more are found elsewhere.) Lastly, Wakeling listed ninety-three sales of two kinds of musical property, first, the stock of music publishers—multiple copies, plates, copyrights, and so on—and secondly, the stock of a few music dealers such as Calkin & Budd. I have ignored these sale-catalogues of property, not because they are to be despised, but because they have nothing to do with the collector proper. In their own right, however, they would form the subject of a new and certainly rewarding bibliographical study.

While I have examined some of the catalogues of anonymous sales—in connection with prices—I shall not consider them in detail. For my general purpose, they lack the interest of association with a person who may have had some position or distinction in the world of music. But in passing I may say that some of these anonymous 'amateur' or 'professorial' collections show such an outstanding breadth of taste and interest that it would be well worth while to undertake research to try to identify their owners. From 1900—the date at which Wakeling's abstract ends—up to 1960, the number of important collectors whose music was sold in part or whole is twenty-five. Besides the sale-catalogues in the British Museum, there are also a few in other public and private libraries. These bring to just over 230 the total of named collections proper which were auctioned or otherwise dispersed. Excepting some in America, I have scrutinised all these catalogues. Various others, mostly early, are known to have existed, but no copies can now be traced. Fortunately, the contents of several are summarised in contemporary sources.

But sale-catalogues are by no means the only source of information, although they are by far the largest one. A few other collectors are known from manuscript or printed catalogues, and from references in periodicals, etc., though the music has mostly long since been dispersed. Others, again, to a total of over fifty scattered over the last three-and-a-half centuries, have given, bequeathed or sold their collections in part or whole to learned institutions.

In the period up to about 1830, I shall mention all collectors whose libraries are more or less fully known. After that date the great increase in the number compels me to treat them selectively. I shall allude briefly to those collections which have been preserved by gift, bequest or purchase, especially when a catalogue or fairly detailed description exists in print. But I may enlarge on the character or significance of certain collectors, if either seems not to have been fully appreciated.

I propose to exclude royal collectors of music, because I have described them elsewhere.[1] Even without them my final total amounts to over 190

[1] 'The Royal Music Library', *The Book Collector* (Autumn, 1958), vol. VII, no. 3, pp. 241–52. Reprinted as Appendix A 1, below, p. 103.

names, which must be presented in a systematic order, particularly because I have interpreted 'music' in the widest possible sense, to include not solely *musica practica*, but also theory, literature and association items. One possible basis of arrangement would have been the *floruit* of the collector, but this is a point not always easy to determine. Another, though more arbitrary, method could have been a grouping by period and type. On balance, it proved best to observe one simple chronological order, based as far as possible on the date of sale, gift or bequest. An auction by no means always takes place at decease: it may be held either in the collector's lifetime, or many years after his death. The exceptions I have had to make to the chronological principle, chiefly in the twentieth century, are not many and are easily explained by the circumstances.

Even this survey, wide as it may seem, does not present the full tale of British collectors. For there were others, besides those known from all the sources I have described, who formed collections, some probably, and others certainly, of very great historical interest. Some came under the hammer, but no copy of the catalogue survives, and it is known only from casual mention by a later collector or by an auctioneer. There were others, again, whose music does not seem to have been auctioned, but simply melted away. Yet they all contributed to the great river of music-collecting which swelled to a flood in the later nineteenth century. I shall mention a few of the earliest of these ghostly collectors in their chronological place. The rest of these sad phantoms, some thirty in all, I shall try to array before you in my last lecture, in which I shall also say something about prices as they have fluctuated during the last 150 years or so.

This, then, is the picture in its broader features. Those who have preceded me in this field have constructed the outline of the map. These lectures are, so to speak, a survey which will fill in more details. We know the location of most of the larger cities, but the map gives little idea of their size, still less of the position of smaller towns or of the direction of the roads and rivers which link one to another. Perhaps our survey may supply some of these details; it may even help to enlarge the scale of the map. It will certainly add to it the line of some of the hills and valleys that diversify this absorb-ingly interesting terrain.

I have paid tribute to some of the early 'musico-cartographers' (if I may coin the word), especially to those who worked in Cambridge. I must also mention the men who blazed many of the trails for them—the auctioneers. I do not know how much those of the eighteenth and early nineteenth centuries really knew about music. But they carried out the difficult task of cataloguing conscientiously, and usually very intelligently. There are few lapses of the kind perpetrated by a Puttick cataloguer who described lot 178 in the Gwilt sale of 1856 as 'Sextus and other Ancient and Miscellaneous Music'. The auctioneers were often bound to compress a quantity of sym-phonies or concertos into a single lot, which thus became a much larger unit than a lot in the average eighteenth- or nineteenth-century book-sale. Hence the total number of lots may often represent only a fraction of the real size of a musical collection. But these auctioneers frequently showed a flair for music that was unusual, early, or important in other ways, and they would single it out for special mention.

Many of the catalogues of White or Musgrave and the early ones of Puttick & Simpson are notable for their intelligent and rational grouping of lots by classes. This is much more helpful than the later practice of lumping everything together in one alphabetical sequence largely governed by the arbitrary prominence given to one item in a lot. Sometimes, however, the auctioneer disappoints, when he fails to catalogue an important collection as a separate whole, but jumbles it up with 'other properties'. This befell, amongst others, the Moscheles Collection, sold in 1847; and no one can now reconstruct its full extent and splendour. So, too, with some of James Hook's music, sold in 1874 long after his death. Therefore I have regretfully omitted from my survey all but a bare mention of these two collectors and of others who were similarly treated. Thus the auctioneers remain—if I may change my metaphor once more—in the wings, but they should not be forgotten when the actors in this pageant of three-and-a-half centuries begin to move across the stage, as it is now high time for them to do.

Who, then, was the first British collector of music? The answer to this question must depend on what, in this context, we mean by a collector. We cannot, I think, call a man a collector just because he may amass the music of his own country and his own day for performance either by himself or by others. Were this so, any English royal person, nobleman, or country gentleman who ever maintained a musical establishment would, *ipso facto*, qualify as a collector.

For a man to be estimated a true collector, we surely require evidence of something wider and deeper, something which denotes a breadth of outlook, a certain spirit of curiosity and a quest for knowledge of the musical past. For these qualities combine to reach beyond the mere reading of the notes for performance. They are often found linked to the study of musical theory and history. To some extent, taste and connoisseurship may inspire the collecting of music, but, as far as I know, in no way as intensively as they have influenced collectors of books. At the risk of making an obvious statement, I would add that the collector must have a real, personal interest in music. I must therefore exclude such eminent bibliophiles as Lumley, Cotton, Harley, Heber, Huth and Grenville. None of them had any personal interest in music or knowledge of it: they seem to have acquired it either incidentally, or simply for the sake of having the subject represented on their shelves.

The point at which music-collecting began cannot, I think, be defined precisely. It must clearly have depended on the time by which enough music had accumulated, in manuscript or print, to be collected; this factor has naturally varied in different countries. I would hazard a guess that the opportunity to collect came later in Britain than on the Continent, where certainly it was established early in the sixteenth century, if not before. Of course, the historical approach is something that could only develop as musical history developed, and clearly much early collecting, in any country, was of necessity contemporary, or nearly so.

Thus we can begin in the reign of Queen Elizabeth I, for the first man I have found who showed most of the essential qualities of a collector was William Heather. He was born *c.* 1563 and died at Oxford in 1627, having founded the Chair of Music that bears his name, and having bequeathed his books to the Music School. A list of them, probably written soon after the bequest,[1] is headed thus: 'A Catalogue of so many setts of bookes as were given by M^r Doctor Heather to the Vniuersitie of Oxford, at the tyme of his first founding the practice of musick there.' The chief part of this list is divided into eight classes, which show that besides printed English music of his older contemporaries Heather had collected works by Frescobaldi, Sweelinck, and Palestrina, and also possessed some of the anthologies published by Phalèse. He owned some theoretical manuscripts by Elway Bevin, and the now famous set of part-books[2] containing festal Masses by English composers of the early sixteenth century such as Aston, Fayrfax and Taverner.

Whether or not the grouping of the printed part-books was Heather's own, it is most interesting bibliographically. For the manuscript list describes clearly the distinctive binding of each group—'with russet covers and orringe culler strings', 'in white velame books with greene strings', 'in white velame covers, having blewe strings' and so on. This suggests that there was a deliberate distinction of colour and material, for two probable purposes—to make each set easy to find on the shelf, and to prevent the books of any one set being confused after use with those of any other. If not Heather himself, someone associated with him showed a collector's instinct in caring for his music. But we know that Heather insisted that his books, and the instruments which he bequeathed with them, be properly checked; for in the *Statuta antiqua Universitatis Oxoniensis*[3] we read: 'Lastlie I ordain that once every yeare the instruments bee viewed, and the bookes: and that neyther of these be lent abroad uppon any pretence whatsoever, nor removed out of the Schoole and place appointed.'

There is no Cambridge counterpart to William Heather. But John Cosin,

---

[1] Bodleian, MS. Mus. Sch. c. 204★.

[2] Now known as the Forrest–Heather part-books (Bodleian, MSS. Mus. Sch. e. 376–81) from the name of William Forrest, Chaplain to Queen Mary, who added the last seven Masses in the books.

[3] Ed. Strickland Gibson (Oxford, 1931), p. 556.

Bishop of Durham from 1660 to 1672, and Master of Peterhouse from 1634 to 1644 and again in 1660, deserves at least an honourable mention, if not a *proxime accessit*. For he was a great bibliophile, and was also interested in music. It is recorded that the copy of Bill's *Book of Common Prayer* (1634) now in Peterhouse Library was interleaved with musical settings written at his request for use in the Chapel.[1] He had musical friends, who gave an organ 'that the scholars might practise music in the Parlour'.[2] It also seems certain that Cosin brought with him from Durham (where he was a pre-bendary before his election to Peterhouse) some of the music in the Peterhouse part-books.[3] It is at least possible that he caused to be brought together the other music (principally from Henry VIII's time) in these books, which are the slightly later equivalent of the Forrest–Heather books. Cosin may then be regarded as a likely begetter of a small collection of great importance, even if he did not assemble all of it himself.[4]

Collectors of this period were to be found not solely in academic circles, but also among the country gentlemen. Edward Paston (1550–1630), second son of Sir Thomas Paston, was a man noted for his musicianship and his skill in the liberal sciences. From his will we know that he possessed a substantial collection of music, including 'lute bookes prickt in ciphers after the Spanish and Italian fashion, and some in A.B.C. according to the English fashion...bound in very good bookes'. Some had voice-parts attached. He also had printed and manuscript books 'of lattin, ffrench and Italian songs, some of three, foure, five, six, seaven, and eight parts'. Some idea of the large size of his collection can be gleaned from the fact that it was stored in three different places in his house—a chest, a closet, and 'fower truncks'.[5]

[1] See T. A. Walker, *Peterhouse* (Cambridge, 1935), p. 70 n. 1.    [2] See Walker, *ibid.* p. 57.
[3] See Dom Anselm Hughes, *Catalogue of the Musical Manuscripts at Peterhouse, Cambridge* (Cambridge, 1953), pp. x–xii. See also Walker, *op. cit.* pp. 128, 131; Peter le Huray, 'Towards a definitive Study of Pre-Restoration Anglican Service Music', *Musica Disciplina*, vol. XIV (1960), p. 180.
[4] Le Huray, *op. cit.* pp. 181–5, points out that, a little later than Cosin, Henry May, a Fellow of Pembroke College, Cambridge, caused a similar collection of church music to be assembled for that College.
[5] For further details see Philip Brett, 'The English Consort Song', *Proceedings of the Royal Musical Association*, session 88 (1961–2), pp. 83–5. Three of the lute books (B.M. Add. MS. 31992, R.C.M. MS. 2089, and Tenbury MS. 340) and one set of part-books (Tenbury MSS. 341–4) have survived. (Two of these are possibly those found as lot 516 in the catalogue of the Williams sale of 1821.) Brett alludes to other possible survivals of Paston manuscripts.

Another important collector of this period was Thomas Hamond (d. 1662) of Hawksdon, near Bury St Edmunds, whose manuscript music, mostly copied between 1631 and 1656, is fortunately preserved almost complete in the Wight Collection in the Bodleian. As Margaret Crum has described it in an admirable article,[1] I need only say here that Hamond's interest in music extended from as far back as Tallis up to his own contemporaries, such as Tomkins. Hamond also owned a few manuscripts now in the British Museum. (Pl. I a.) There were certainly other collectors in the earlier part of the seventeenth century (for instance, the Filmer family: see p. 89), but they are at present shadowy figures, and it is only with the emergence of John Evelyn, Samuel Pepys and Thomas Britton that the variety of our pageant grows apace and the horizons of collecting begin to expand.

From his diary we know that Evelyn was all his life a keen amateur of music, more perhaps as an observer and listener than as a player. None of his biographers seems to mention the fact that he owned a small but choice collection of music, of which his autograph catalogue is extant in the Evelyn Collection at Christ Church (*Catalogus Evelynianus 1687*, MS. 20ª, p. 190). It comprises twenty-nine items, mostly printed Italian madrigals of the late sixteenth and early seventeenth century, and including also some interesting manuscripts and theory. Among the former were 'Recitativas from ye Opera at Venice 1646' and 'some excellent compositions of ye great masters of the Opera at Venice 1646', both presumably acquired, as may have been some of the printed music, during Evelyn's travels.

It is Evelyn's diary that gives us information about an otherwise unknown collection, which met an unusual fate. The entry for 25 November 1695 mentions the scientist and inventor Sir Samuel Moreland, and states: 'He had newly buried 200 pounds worth of music books as he sayd. 6 foote under grounde, as being love songs and vanity.' In the event, Moreland buried his music books not long before he himself was buried, for he died on 30 December 1695. It is perhaps worth noting that Evelyn owned a copy

---

[1] 'A Seventeenth Century Collection of Music belonging to Thomas Hamond, a Suffolk Landowner', *The Bodleian Library Record* (Oct. 1957), vol. VI, no. 1, pp. 373–86.

of Moreland's rare pamphlet, *Tuba stentoro-phonica* (Godbid, 1671) in which he described the speaking trumpet of his own invention.

The music which Samuel Pepys collected and which ultimately passed, with the rest of his incomparable library, to Magdalene College, Cambridge in 1724, is an extraordinary mixture. Although the exact quantity is not yet known, it probably amounts to rather more than eighty items, manuscript and printed, consisting partly or wholly of music, and falling into two broad categories. The first, and larger, comprises music in which Pepys had, or could have had, some personal interest—works for his own special instruments, the flageolet and recorder, both of his own day and of an earlier generation: songs and guitar music in the hand of, or associated with, Cesare Morelli, his private musician: operas by such composers as Lanciano, Alessandro Scarlatti and Cesti. Some thirty items consist of works on theory and instruments. The second group contains manuscripts of a much earlier date, such as no. 1236, an important source of English church music, *c.* 1490: no. 1760, a collection of secular chansons by Netherlands composers made for Prince Arthur (d. 1502): no. 1594, which contains songs by Machaut. But as Pepys had no knowledge of early music, he can only have acquired these books—like so many others in his collection—because they aroused his curiosity. Whether or not he bought on the suggestion of some unknown musical adviser, posterity has cause to bless his flair for the unusual.

Britton, the dealer in 'small-coal', who gave weekly concerts at his house in Clerkenwell from 1678 to 1714, free at first, later for a nominal 10*s.* a year, is too famous a figure in English music to need description here. Hawkins gives all the details, and reprints verbatim the sale-catalogue of his music, providentially so, as no copy of the original is now known. Ward, the auctioneer who sold the collection after Britton had been frightened to death by a ventriloquist in September 1714, neatly said that he was the 'most valuable man that ever enjoyed so harmonious a life in so low a station', and went on: 'there is not a book or instrument mentioned here that is not his own: and as it will be the best sale that hath been made in its kind, so it shall be the fairest'. Britton seems to have been something of a bibliophile, for

Ward emphasised that many of the books were 'neatly bound...the whole being carefully preserved in admirable order'. There were 212 lots, of which 160 were instrumental. The European range of the collection back to about 1620 for the French, Italian and German music and to Tallis for the English, is amazing. Some of the works are now quite unknown. What, for instance, is 'Romolo's two choirs in six books'? Britton's extensive general library, sold in 1169 lots, with a strong emphasis on science and philosophy, contained works on musical theory and some psalm-books.

It is most important to note that Britton's sale included twenty-seven lots of instruments, at least half being much earlier than his own lifetime. It is the first known sale from which a detailed description of them survives, though we have seen that Heather, too, collected instruments as well as music. Another early collector of both, hitherto unknown, was Robert Orme. The sale of his musical property took place on 20 December 1711, 'at the new House next the Wheat-Sheaf, in Henrietta Street'. The announcement in *The Daily Courant* describes it as consisting of 'Cremona-Violins, Ross, and Jay-Viols, Flutes, Hautbois, Guitarrs, Lutes and Harpsychords, made by the best hands: together with an excellent collection of books of musick, containing the choicest sonatas, motetts, aires, etc.' Examination of later sale-catalogues right up to the eighteen-nineties shows that at least seventy per cent of the collectors of music also collected instruments, often of great historical interest, on which to re-create their treasures of manuscript and print. The relation between the collector, his music and his instruments is a fascinating topic, as yet I believe quite unexplored, but one on which I cannot enlarge in these lectures.

Pepys, the diarist, naval administrator, observer of human nature; Britton, the 'small-coal man', the student of alchemy and the occult—what a splendidly contrasting pair they make! In their sharp distinction, how bravely they typify and anticipate the even greater variety of collectors to come during the later eighteenth century and the nineteenth! As this pageant proceeds, it will unfold a fascinating diversity of musical character and interest—the performer or concert promoter with recondite historical tastes;

the scholar who used his treasures for editorial or historical purposes; the sentimentalist who simply revered the great masters; the singer and the executant with a vast library, who edited nothing; the composer of small merit who showed a taste for the unexpected or collected with a striking vision of grandeur; the professor who based lectures upon his collection; the publisher who strengthened an inherited archive; the amateur who, though apparently devoid of special musical training, developed a flair for acquiring rarities; the plain man whose music, while of no special distinction in itself, has acquired it through some quirk of circumstance or history; and, of course, the specialists. This rich diversity of collectors is matched by the range of music collected. For the permutations of type, period and origin seem to be almost infinite. As in literature, so in music, to an extent not yet perhaps fully realised,

> non unus vitae color est, nec carminis unus
> lector: habet tempus pagina quaeque suum.

Now we are on the threshold of the Georgian era, and collectors begin to multiply. But we meet an early disappointment, namely the library of 'Thomas Ravenscroft' listed by Deutsch as having been sold in 1709. This collection, unfortunately, had nothing to do with the Stuart composer who died in about 1633. For it contains practically no music, but is a large general library, with books on philosophy and the like printed as late as 1708. The title-page of the sale-catalogue describes the owner as 'Thomas Ravenscroft Esqre', with no mention that he was a musician. The Ravenscrofts were quite a numerous family, and this must be another Thomas Ravenscroft, the one who died on 20 April 1708.[1]

But some other collections of the early eighteenth century still survive, real and intact. In 1710 Christ Church, Oxford, received by bequest the first of the two music libraries[2] that fell to them in this period, when at Dean Aldrich's death his rich collection of compositions, printed and manuscript,

---

[1] See W. Ravenscroft, *Some Ravenscrofts* (Milford-on-Sea, 1929), p. 49.

[2] The Rawlinson Collection, the third mentioned by Deutsch, consists of only six volumes of music, a mere drop in the ocean of manuscripts which this 'topographer and non-juring bishop' (D.N.B.) bequeathed to the Bodleian in 1755.

by Tudor and Stuart composers, was added to its treasures. In 1718 the same foundation received the smaller collection of the elder Richard Goodson, Professor of Music from 1682 to 1718. The music books collected by each man can be identified from the good manuscript catalogue made by J. B. Malchair in July 1787, now in the Royal College of Music.[1] It gives many most interesting details about condition, shelving and binding, and shows that in general Goodson was more interested in music of the mid and later seventeenth century, Aldrich in that of the more remote past. Goodson's collection was considerably the smaller of the two, occupying only fifteen folios in Malchair's hand, compared with the fifty-two needed for Aldrich. Malchair's task of cataloguing was clearly a lengthy one, and it is not perhaps surprising that he sometimes faltered, and lapsed into what are now inelegantly called 'blanket' entries, such as '8 books in a bundle, all lumber probably'. In his will (quoted in the preface to Arkwright's catalogue) Aldrich requested the Dean and Chapter 'to take care of my prints and books of musick, that they may not be exposed to common usage... because they are things of value in themselves and to be found in very few libraries'. His music makes an interesting study in the light of his weekly music meetings.[2]

One who took an active part in these meetings was Narcissus Marsh (1638–1713), the famous bibliophile and ecclesiastic, who was a Fellow of Exeter College and Principal of St Alban's Hall from 1673 to 1678, when he was elected Provost of Trinity College, Dublin. Later he became successively Bishop of Ferns and Leighlin, and Archbishop of Cashel, of Dublin and Armagh. In his diary[3] Marsh wrote

I had before this [1664], betaken myself to the practise of musick, especially of the viol, and after the fire of London I constantly kept a weekly consort (of instrumental musick, & sometimes vocal), on Wednesday, in the afternoon, & then on Thursday, as long as I lived in Oxford. This I did as an exercise, using no other; but labouring harder at my study all the rest of the week.

[1] R.C.M. MS. 2125.
[2] See W. G. Hiscock, *Henry Aldrich of Christ Church* (Oxford, 1960), pp. 32–41: also p. 4 and p. 13, on his music-collecting. Hiscock gives '8,000 works of music' as the total of this section of Aldrich's library.
[3] Partly printed in the *Irish Ecclesiastical Journal* (Dublin, 1886), vol. v.

Marsh was a good enough theoretician to write 'An Essay touching the (esteemed) sympathy between Lute or Viol Strings'.[1] His very fine collection of music comprised both vocal and instrumental works, English and foreign, of the late sixteenth and early seventeenth centuries. At his death in 1713 it passed to the famous library of his own foundation in Dublin.

Another bequest came in the seventeen-forties, when the north of England was greatly enriched by the music left to Durham Cathedral by Philip Falle, who was a Canon of Durham from 1699 to 1742. The catalogue mentioned in his bequest has unfortunately disappeared, but it seems reasonable to assume that a good deal of the very important early music published by Gardano, Scotto, Phalèse, Geertsom, Le Cène and Playford and now in the Cathedral Library, was collected by him. The total is upwards of 300 items. Nothing is known of Falle's musical interests.

Two other notable collections of this era were sold, but no copy of either sale-catalogue has come to light. Of the composer William Corbett's library, sold about 1750, nothing is known save the fact that he collected most of it during his sojourn in Italy. Hawkins, who tells us this,[2] says he was 'a great collector', adding that when in Italy 'besides his salary he had an allowance from the government', and that 'his business in Rome was to watch the motions of the Pretender'. Concerning Pepusch's great antiquarian collection, mostly dispersed at his death in 1752, we can infer something from the very high quality of those items which reappear in later sales. He owned many treasures besides the Fitzwilliam Virginal Book, and fortunately a list of some of them has been preserved in John Ward's *Lives of the Professors of Gresham College*.[3] This list, which occurs in the chapter on John Bull, is a transcript of a small part of Pepusch's own catalogue. Though devoted to Bull's music, this selection enables one to identify some notable virginal manuscripts, three being in the hand of Messaeus: one of them is now B.M. Add. MS. 23623 and another Paris Conservatoire MS. Rés. 1186.

---

[1] Summarised, with the above title, in Robert Plot's *Natural History of Oxford-Shire* (Oxford, 1677), pp. 289–99. For other points in Marsh's musical activity see W. G. Hiscock, *op. cit.* pp. 32–3; and Anthony à Wood, *Life and Times*, ed. Arthur Clark (Oxford, 1891), vol. I, pp. 274–5.

[2] *A General History of Music* (London, 1853), p. 823.      [3] London, 1740, pp. 203–8.

The highest volume number quoted in this list is 131, which gives some idea of the considerable size of Pepusch's collection.

We might have learned a good deal more about Pepusch's library from the libraries of Ephraim Kelner and John Travers, sold in 1763 and 1766 respectively, for to each of them he bequeathed a part of his books. But here, too, no catalogue is known. One authority states that he left the most valuable part of his collection to the Academy of Ancient Music[1] but again no list is extant. So Pepusch, as a collector, must remain a shadowy figure. We know, however, that he supervised the Duke of Chandos's music collection when he was in charge of the band at Cannons. For in 1720 Pepusch himself checked and signed the catalogue made by a Mr Noland.[2] The Duke's collection, typical perhaps of a nobleman's interests at this date, amounted to 129 items, from Purcell onwards, including Campra, Colasse, Bassani, Handel, and, not unnaturally, Pepusch.

In 1759 occurred the death of Handel. Though no collector himself— provident as he was in preserving his own autographs—he deserves mention here as the unwitting begetter of much of the specialised collecting ever done in these islands. Many of the numerous copies made in his lifetime for utilitarian purposes became the pride of such noble families as the Granvilles, Aylesfords, Malmesburys and Shaftesburys. Some of these copies still remain in family possession; some have passed to libraries; others have been eagerly sought as they have come up at auction. Such is the famous group of sixty-seven volumes of J. C. Smith copies of Handel, owned successively by Thomas Greatorex, John Ireland, Dean of Westminster, and Henry Barrett Lennard, and presented in 1902 by the latter's son to the Fitzwilliam Museum.

The time of the general Handel collector did not come until well into the nineteenth century, with one notable but rather obscure exception. Nichols records in his *Literary Anecdotes* (vol. III, p. 739) one John Walkden, who died at Windsor in 1808 and may therefore be presumed to have been active

---

[1] See the article by the Rev. Charles Mackeson on the Academy in *Grove*, 1st to 4th editions, derived presumably from Hawkins, p. 908.

[2] Cf. C. H. Collins Baker and M. I. Baker, *The Life and Circumstances of James Brydges, First Duke o Chandos* (Oxford, 1949), pp. 132–9.

not very long after Handel's death. Walkden was a stationer in Shoe Lane, and from his business 'acquired a handsome fortune with an unexceptionable character'. Nichols goes on: 'He was passionately fond of Handel's music, of which he possessed a sufficient quantity to make a sale of six days. At his house in Highbury Place he built a very spacious music room, in which he placed a bust of Handel over an excellent organ, on which he was a complete performer.' It is a thousand pities that no record of such a big sale (perhaps the first consisting wholly of the music of one composer) can now be traced.

Shortly after Handel's death, Robert, Lord Clive (whose musical interests seem unknown to his biographers) began to build up a collection of quite exceptional scope and distinction. His wife, his daughter Charlotte, and other relatives and descendants shared his enthusiasm. By the early nineteenth century, it had grown to over 160 volumes, comprising English, French, Spanish and Portuguese vocal music in manuscript, from Gibbons to Mysliveček, and well over 200 works, largely instrumental, by composers of many nations published in London. It is perhaps significant of the Clive family's taste that Schobert bulked much larger than Handel. The collection remained intact until 1948, when it was dispersed.[1]

Rather different in character was the collection made by the Cornewall family of Moccas Court, Herefordshire, which has almost entirely vanished. Fortunately a detailed and most interesting manuscript catalogue, dated 1796 and now owned by Albi Rosenthal, has survived. This was predominantly a vocal collection, amounting to about 2000 items, with some Italian bias, but besides Alessandro Scarlatti and Jomelli it extended to Gluck. A special section of the catalogue, dated 1795, contained music belonging to a Miss Cornewall, who also owned R.C.M. MSS. 2061–4. The exact ownership of the printed organ and harpsichord music, some 400 pieces in all, is not stated. But it is a good deal wider in range than the songs, and included, besides Domenico Scarlatti and Avison, works by W. F. E. Bach, Boccherini, Corelli, Haydn (in large quantities), Mozart

[1] A detailed description of it was given by A. Rosenthal Ltd in their catalogue no. 10.

and Beethoven. To collect, in 1796, such a modern composer as Beethoven, for inclusion in a library reaching back to the Scarlattis, argues a family with both enterprise and historical feeling. Three manuscripts[1] in the British Museum can be associated with Frances Elizabeth Cornewall, who in 1805 became the wife of Henry Fleming Lea, fourteenth Viscount Hereford. A certain A. M. Cornewall owned R.C.M. MS. 428. These are the only surviving evidence I have found of this family of collectors. But none can be identified for certain with items in the manuscript catalogue.

Even greater in quality and extent was the collection built up by Sir Watkin Williams-Wynn, the fourth baronet (d. 1789), and continued by other members of the family. When I inspected it at Wynnstay in 1945, it lay in a stable, a huge mound of music ruined by damp, but splendid even in its mouldering decay. It was practically all unbound, mint, in wrappers, as issued. The bulk was English, back to the seventeen-thirties, but it also included many Hummel and Roger editions, besides some French and Austrian publications. But only a fraction of the pile could be rescued, as a pathetic witness to Sir Watkin's breadth of musical interests. How many other eighteenth-century collections, as shown by the recurrence of great names in subscribers' lists, must have met an equally sad end, through fire or neglect!

As so many treasures of the majority of the great eighteenth-century collectors have either perished or been dispersed, it is all the more gratifying that at Burghley House near Stamford, the seat of the Marquis of Exeter, a small but notable library survives intact. Probably assembled by Cecil Brownlow, ninth Earl of Burghley (1725–93), it amounts to some sixty volumes of manuscript, and several hundred printed items, comprising mainly German and English vocal music of the period, as well as some Italian instrumental music. Much of the collection is in excellent condition. The ninth Earl was a performer as well as a collector: he possessed an organ shaped like a harpsichord, which is still in the chapel at Burghley House.

In 1764 there was sold at Standlinch, near Salisbury, by an auctioneer

[1] Add. 31665; 31639, ff. 45–49*b*; 31516, ff. 42–83.

named Prestage, the collection of William Young, who was 'going abroad'. Its 449 lots comprised a remarkable assemblage of every kind of music, including many manuscripts, far beyond what a cultivated country gentleman would require for daily performance, from operas by Vinci to keyboard works by Mondonville and Scarlatti. There were also eight volumes of concertos by 'Piantanida', which raises an interesting point, for of the three north Italian composers of this name known to Eitner, none is credited with any concertos. This is a good example of the quantity of secondary music of the eighteenth century that has apparently just vanished—unless the *International Inventory of Musical Sources* brings it to light.

In the seventeen-seventies there were but two sales of outstanding collections—Gostling and Boyce. The Gostling Collection was sold in 1777 by Langford, who headed the title-page of the catalogue: 'Bibliotheca Musicae Reconditae Eximiaeque Locuples' and went on, on page 4: 'whatever was wanting to render the collection complete…was supplied by the late owner' and continued: 'upon the whole, it may with truth be asserted, that an entire collection of music, equal to this in respect of originality, variety, or those circumstances of selection that distinguish it, in this country at least, has never been brought to public sale, in memory of any person living'. This high claim was surely justified, because the collection had been begun by the famous bass John Gostling (born *c.* 1650), who was for some time a sub-dean of St Paul's Cathedral, and for whom Purcell wrote some notable solo parts. It was continued by his son William Gostling, a minor canon of Canterbury Cathedral. The latter added some music given to him by William Raylton, an organist of that cathedral from 1736 to 1757. The collection thus built up over a period of nearly 100 years amounted to 173 lots, with an average of eight or nine items in a lot. It was exceptionally rich in English and Italian music of the late sixteenth and early seventeenth centuries, and included quantities of anthems in score. It was distinguished by such rarities as the first edition of *Parthenia*, Robinson's *Schoole of Musick*, an imperfect copy of Day's 'Service of 1565' (presumably *Certaine Notes*), Dutch psalms in manuscript and works by Le Jeune, La Barre, and Sweelinck. Lot 18 perhaps deserves quotation: it simply reads 'Loosemore's five Bell Concert', an intriguing and mysterious title. No such work by any of the three Loosemores now seems to be known.

If the Gostling Collection reflects the interest of pure collectors, the music assembled by William Boyce, and sold in 1778 by Christie in 266 lots, is noteworthy because it shows how widely one who was a successful composer could develop his acquisitive taste. The sale-catalogue is not, unfortunately, always very clear, and not all the music can now be identified. But happily nearly a score of the lots (including Alessandro Scarlatti's *Sinfonie* and the Cosyn Virginal book) can be safely recognised, through the name of the purchaser 'Nicolay',[1] as now being in the Royal Music Library. Boyce plainly had a taste for the antique and the curious, with a strong bias towards Italian music of the sixteenth and early seventeenth centuries. He had, for instance, not only a good deal of Palestrina and of his lesser contemporaries and successors, but also a manuscript score of Victoria's motets, and several operas by Lully.

The collection of the blind organist and distinguished composer John Stanley, sold by Christie in 1786, was neither large, comprising only fifty-four lots of music, nor marked by anything unusual. The cataloguing was often brief to the point of obscurity, as in the lot simply described as 'Comus and various'! But the collection raises an interesting point. How did Stanley, blinded at the age of two, study his music? Did someone play it for him to memorise? He also had works of musical reference, such as Grassineau's dictionary and, incidentally, his other books included Herodotus, works by John Locke, and the plays of Farquhar and Plautus! (Stanley's bookplate, which includes his signature (Pl. II*a*), is found in BM. Add. MSS. 5329-32, 5324-6.)

Edmund Thomas Warren, later Warren-Horne, part of whose collection was auctioned by Leigh & Sotheby in 1797, was secretary of the Noblemen and Gentlemen's Catch Club from 1761 to 1794 and a publisher and editor

---

[1] See my article: 'Portrait of a Bibliophile. V. Frederick Nicolay, 1728/29–1809', *The Book Collector* (Winter, 1960), pp. 401–13 (reprinted as Appendix A 2, below, p. 115).

of repute. His music and musical literature made up 157 lots, which included numerous English madrigals in score, fancies by Orlando Gibbons and Ferrabosco, five books of concertos for the flute, and two large volumes of cantatas by Porpora and Scarlatti. Besides these, lot 101 deserves mention —'Proof sheets of old music, for an intended publication, but never executed, the only copy in the world, plates being destroyed and no other copy ever taken'.

This volume (bought by 'Read' for £1. 1s.) is now in the British Museum.[1] It has a long, interesting note in Horne's hand, explaining that these plates were prepared in January 1777 as the first of six volumes each of one hundred plates. The reason for non-completion was that the publisher Mary Welcker broke her agreement, and never sent back the plates. All that Horne ever received was the uncorrected proofs of his first volume, which her executors returned to him in April 1782, after her death. The music is most interesting, and embraces works from Heinrich Isaac and Pierre de la Rue to John Bennet. Here plainly was a late eighteenth-century equivalent of the historical anthology of Davison and Apel, and, by intention at least, it gives England as much international priority in this special field as did Arnold's Handel in that of the collected edition. A second portion of Horne's music was sold in 1810.[2]

The music library amassed by William and Philip Hayes is remarkable for several reasons, besides its quality. To my knowledge it is the first and only collection of music made by two brothers, and the only one of this period sold not by auction but by means of a catalogue with printed prices. The exact date of the sale is not known. But as the copy of the catalogue in the British Museum is watermarked 1797 and as Philip Hayes died in that year—William pre-deceased him—the date may be put with some probability in or shortly after 1798. In any case, it was before 1805, because 'Smart's Music Warehouse' (in which the music was deposited) ceased to exist after

[1] Pressmark: K.7.i.12.
[2] Horne was an indefatigable maker of manuscript copies: thirteen large B.M. Add. MSS. (14398, 29386, 30309, 31121, 31393, 31409, 31418, 31442, 31462, 31463, 31490, 31805, 34071) and R.C.M. MSS. 517, 571, 668, 1025, 1092, 4075 (twelve volumes) are wholly or partly in his hand. This list is by no means exhaustive.

that year. The collection, in the words of the title-page, comprised music 'by Tallis, Tye, Child, Gibbons...and more than three hundred and fifty Italian, English, German and French composers, the greatest part in excellent preservation, and collected through a series of years, with infinite care and judgment'. It was grouped in 543 well-classified lots, and did indeed cover every type of music by almost every composer of note from Tye to Haydn, excepting J. S. Bach and his sons. In connection with this library, I cannot refrain from quoting the immortal remark enshrined in Husk's article in *Grove* (printed in the text from the first edition to the fourth, but relegated to a footnote in the fifth): 'Dr P. Hayes was one of the largest men in England...He is buried in St Paul's Cathedral.' Whether William Hayes was of a similarly heroic stature, I do not know, but the catalogue of their noble library shows that both brothers had collected on an heroic scale.

The other great event of 1798 was the sale of the library of Thomas Bever (1725–91), Doctor of Laws, judge of the Cinque Ports, Chancellor of Lincoln and Bangor, and Fellow of All Souls. No copy of the catalogue is recorded, but providentially it is summarised in *The Gentleman's Magazine*[1] as follows:

On June 7 and 8 were sold by Mr White at Storey's Gate, Westminster, the very choice and valuable musical library of the late Dr Bever...who bequeathed it to Mr John Hindle[2] by order of whose administratrix it was now disposed of...the whole in fine preservation, obtained and purchased with great judgment and indefatigable pains at considerable expense, during a long course of years.

The composers named in this summary make it clear that Bever's taste ran especially to the Italians of the late sixteenth and seventeenth centuries. (A note of ownership in his hand, with his bookplate, is reproduced in Pl. III.) Any item from his library was highly prized by later generations. Some fine pieces are in the manuscript collections of the British Museum, the Royal College of Music, and in the Fitzwilliam Collection, of which the 1894 catalogue states that Bever employed a copyist named Robert Dids-

---

[1] Vol. LXVIII, p. 517.
[2] 1761–96, a minor composer, who is also known as a copyist of part of B.M. Add. MS. 15979: cf. Hughes-Hughes, vol. II, p. 310.

bury, who seems to have put into score much music from early part-books. Bever was a friend of Burney[1] and, at some time before July 1771, had composed an oratorio *Hercules*, now in the Bodleian.[2]

The last collection of music auctioned in the eighteenth century belonged to Samuel Howard. He is probably identical with the pupil of Pepusch who was a composer of songs and cantatas and graduated Mus.D. at Cambridge in 1769. Howard's collection, sold seventeen years after his death by White in 1799, in 156 lots, was rather poorly catalogued. But sufficient detail is given to show that it reflects sound judgement and some catholicity of interest. Besides a goodly array of fantasias by such composers as Coperario, Gibbons, Lawes and Locke, Howard owned a copy of Scheidt's *Tabulatura Nova* and Le Jeune's *Psalms* in the Paris edition of 1650. His liking for the early seventeenth century is clearly marked: the manuscripts included a 'copy' of Elway Bevin's Canons, possibly the autograph now in the Royal Music Library; at the other extreme Howard possessed the symphonies of the Landgrave of Hesse.

The end of the eighteenth century was not, of course, the end of the eighteenth-century tradition of collecting music. Not a few of Samuel Howard's younger contemporaries lived on into the new era. The greatest of them, Burney, Hawkins, Bartleman, Lord Fitzwilliam and Edward Jones, had made their name while George III and Queen Charlotte were still building up the music in the Royal Library. Excepting Hawkins, they all went on adding to their treasures throughout the Regency.

They were, perhaps, the last of the connoisseurs, whose line reaches back to William Heather. Together, they form an episode in this pageant which is too magnificent to be presented as a crowded appendage to the seventeen-nineties. To appreciate its full dignity and grandeur, we must see these five collectors and their lesser contemporaries against the more spacious background of the early nineteenth century. With this I propose to begin my second lecture.

---

[1] See P. A. Scholes, *The Great Dr Burney* (London, 1948), vol. I, p. 191, and Bever's autograph note in his copy of Trabacci's *Secondo libro de ricercate*, now in the British Museum.

[2] MS. music, b.13: see J. H. Mee, *The Oldest Music Room in Europe* (London, 1911), p. 32.

# LECTURE II

# THE GREATER GEORGIANS AND THE LESSER VICTORIANS: 1800 TO 1849

The dawn of the nineteenth century brings two bequests; first, of the outstanding collection formed by the Rev. Osborne Wight, and, second, of the music amassed by the redoubtable General John Reid. Wight was a Fellow of New College and bequeathed his collection to the Bodleian in 1801. Besides some printed works, he had collected over 209 manuscripts of Italian and English vocal music of the seventeenth and early eighteenth century, including the Hamond manuscripts mentioned on p. 10.[1] In addition to these he had much other music, which he left to a 'Mr Swanton', who cannot now be traced. A good deal of Wight's collection came from Hayes, and a score or so volumes from J. Awbery, another Fellow of New College.

The Reid Library, which was bequeathed to Edinburgh University in 1806, is noteworthy as the earliest known library of music formed in Scotland. The remarkable circumstances of the General's life have been admirably summarised by the present Reid Librarian, Jean Allan,[2] and so need no further description here. His bequest of 'all his music books to the Professor of Music in that college' was made subject to his daughter retaining them during her life, so that they did not actually pass to the University until she died, in 1838. It is unfortunate that no list of the bequest has survived. Only five books, mostly comprising music for flute—the General's favourite instrument—can be identified today. But the old core of this famous library must contain many more.

---

[1] The manuscripts are described in vol. IV of the *Summary Catalogue of Western Manuscripts in the Bodleian Library* (Oxford, 1897), pp. 1–36. Some details of Wight's life and character are given in the *Gentleman's Magazine* for 1800, p. 1212.

[2] 'The Reid Music Library, University of Edinburgh: its Origin and Friends', *Library World*, vol. LI (1948), pp. 99–101.

## Georgians and Victorians, 1800 to 1849

During the later part of the eighteenth century there were active a number of minor collectors, whose music was sold between 1800 and 1830. They deserve brief mention, if only for the sake of completeness, in this important period. The first and lesser part of William Kitchiner's large collection, which was sold in 1809, can be most conveniently considered with the larger portion, auctioned after his decease in 1838. In 1811 Sotheby sold the music library of Henry Compton, who resided at St James's Palace and must have made music with Frederick Nicolay, being, like him, a Page of the Back Stairs to Queen Charlotte. Compton specialised in instrumental works of the early and mid eighteenth century, especially tutors. One lot, comprising fifty-nine such instruction books, sold for only 9s. Methods and tutors also loomed large in the collection of John Sydney of Hunton in Kent, sold by Sotheby in 1813 in 740 lots. He owned a copy of the *Instructions for Playing on the Musical Glasses* (1761), by Anne Ford: perhaps this is the unique copy now in Harvard University Library.

The Rev. John Parker, 'Rector of St George, Botolph Lane', had a good collection of seventeenth-century music, including Italian madrigals. When auctioned by White in 1813, these mostly fetched higher prices than did his copy of Allison's *Psalms* (1599) which made only 1s. and Perrine's *Livre de musique pour le lut* (1679) which went to Timothy Essex for 3s. 6d. In 1814 two interesting collectors come to light, at a double sale by White—'Mr Malchair and Mr Harrison', who were both concerned with music of the early and mid eighteenth century. John Baptist Malchair (1727–1812), the well-known painter in water-colours, was the son of a Cologne watchmaker. He was for many years leader of the famous Oxford Music Room Band, and prominent at the Three Choirs' Festival.[1] Mr Harrison was Samuel Harrison, a famous tenor, who made his name at the Handel Commemoration of 1784. The composer J. B. Cramer sold his music in 1816, forty-two years before he died. The good catalogue, compiled by White, reveals a certain catholicity of interest that might not be expected in so dull

---

[1] His life is recounted in some detail in J. H. Mee, *The Oldest Music Room in Europe* (London, 1911), pp. 79–85. It was Malchair who catalogued the Christ Church music in 1787.

a musician. The collection, in 327 lots, ranged from Amerbach's *Orgel- oder Instrument-Tabulatur* of 1571 (previously owned by J. S. Bach, C. P. E. Bach and Burney and now in Cambridge University Library) to Baltzar's manuscript solos for violin, and a large quantity of Dussek.

The name of Robert Smith is perhaps best known for his good copies of Handel, apparently made in the seventeen-sixties, and now in the Royal Music Library. So it is not surprising that Handel bulked fairly large in his collection which White sold in 276 lots in 1813. This Smith also owned Handel's anthems in a 'MS of Mr Schmidt: gift from the King's Library'. This, incidentally, taken with other hints scattered through the catalogues of the nineteenth century, suggests that George III must have given away quite a lot of his music for one reason or another. Besides Handel, Robert Smith's collection, carefully built up, included a solid core of masses, motets and madrigals, and a large quantity of catches and glees. Although he had very little instrumental music, he did possess a copy of Pevernage's *Harmonia celeste* and, an equal rarity, Gouy's *Pseaumes* of 1650.

The music owned by Henry Harington, glee composer, physician and Mayor of Bath, and founder of the Bath Philharmonic Society, was neither extensive nor generally unusual, but it did include one real gem, of a liturgical rather than of a strictly musical character—a manuscript Horae of the Blessed Virgin Mary, which had belonged to the Cambiaso family of Genoa (Lot 77 in the Sotheby sale of 1816). It was $1\frac{1}{2}$ in. high, 1 in. wide, and was bound in chased gold, inlaid with thirty diamonds. It was purchased by Rodd for £19. 19s. The third sale of 1816 was that of Samuel Webbe's collection. Rather sadly, for a highly successful composer of glees, it included thirty-six lots of his own unpublished MSS.: more surprisingly, he owned the now very rare Breitkopf catalogues for the years 1762 to 1770. The famous glee composer J. W. Callcott sold most of his library in 1819, two years before his death. White's catalogue[1] lists 635 lots of music, mostly of the early and mid eighteenth century, but including a good many theoretical works, French, Italian, German and Spanish.

[1] Copy in Cambridge University Library, L.27.58 (4).

Fifteen smallish collections appear in the eighteen-twenties, all except two with Musgrave as the auctioneer. The library of George Ebenezer Williams, organist of Westminster Abbey (who died in his thirty-seventh year in 1819), was sold by White in 1820, together with the music of 'other eminent professors'. The 600-odd lots included 'two books for the lute. Curious MS. by E. Paston', a copy of Tallis's forty-part motet 'from the original in Lord Oxford's collection', in addition to many notable printed sets of madrigals and motets.

Giuseppe Naldi, the Italian singer and composer, did not become a British subject although he sang regularly in London from 1806 to 1819. (His untimely death, which occurred in 1820, was due to the bursting of an experimental steam cooking-kettle during its trial in the Paris apartment of his friend Garcia.) His collection, auctioned by Oxenham, deserves brief mention as the only foreign one sold in London during the first half of the nineteenth century. The 108 lots of music included a large quantity of Italian opera written from about 1770 onwards. Among his furniture was an un-usual piece made under his own direction—'a composer's pedestal writing desk' with a Broadwood pianoforte built in.

The music of one Henry Hinckley of Guildford Street, London, was sold by Musgrave in 1822; it consisted principally, and rather unusually, of wind pieces. In 1823 we meet the collection of William Dowding, auctioned in 215 lots. It included a copy of the Cianchettini edition of the symphonies of Haydn, Mozart and Beethoven, which, only fourteen years after publica-tion, could be described as 'very scarce'. The reason for this was that, as later revealed by Cianchettini himself,[1] there had been only sixty-two subscribers. Even if only half of the music owned by the Rev. Dr Monk-house, sold with that of 'a distinguished professor' in 1823, were his, it would mark him out as a fine collector. He possessed many now rare part-books of the sixteenth and seventeenth centuries, some good instru-mental music of the latter period, some Jomelli manuscripts and some apparently early copies of Handel. In the catalogue of the Monkhouse

[1] In *The Harmonicon* (July 1827), p. 139.

27

sale we meet that charming word 'airiettes' in the description of lot 91 (cf. p. 45).

In 1824 there was sold the music amassed by William Boyce the younger, in 366 lots. It was a dull collection on the whole, apart from a few items associated with his father, such as lot 86, which comprised 'the words of anthems for Christmas Day and Good Friday, in the handwriting of his late Majesty, King George the Third, and delivered by him to Dr Boyce'.

The collection of the eminent Scottish-born violoncellist John Gunn revealed, when sold in 1824, some good theory and a mass of eighteenth-century church music. This sale included an unusual, separate group of eighteen volumes, 'unpublished scores in MS of various vocal pieces, collected by Mrs Dickons in Italy'. (This was presumably the singer Maria Dickons, *née* Poole, who was a pupil of Rauzzini.) The composers include such now forgotten names as Generali, Guecco, Manfrocce and Tavesi. Dr Jameson of Cheltenham seems to have had a rather undistinguished collection sold, with some other properties, in 1825, but it did include some manuscripts of Carissimi motets, and Carlo Grossi's *Moderne melodie* for voice, strings and organ (Antwerp, 1680).

The music of Mr Sharpe of Knutsford, dispersed in 1825, needs only a bare mention before we pass to that of the glee-composer William Knyvett, who disposed of his library when he moved from London to the country. Musgrave justly said in his preface to the catalogue that 'few if any have displayed a more chaste and judicious selection of the best compositions'. The 274 lots included music which ranged, rather surprisingly perhaps, from Frescobaldi and Victoria to Mozart and Beethoven. From various descriptions in the catalogue, Knyvett seems to have taken some pride in fine bindings.

R. C. Sidney of Mortimer Street, London, owned some good chamber music, sold in 1827. Joseph Gwilt, architect to the Grocers' Company, and editor of a collection of madrigals, lived until 1863, but sold his music in 1828 (with the residue of Naldi's). One interesting item was Clementi's *Introducción a el arte de tocar el pianoforte*: was this printed or manuscript?

The libraries of John Sale and P. Taylor were mixed up in a sale of 1828. It included some good early theory, a collection of music for wind-band in sixteen volumes, and a 'fine' manuscript of Carissimi's *I Naviganti*, which reappears in 1829 as lot 67 in an anonymous sale of 26 September.

By far the most notable sale of the eighteen-twenties was that of the music belonging to the composer William Shield who died in 1829. The 247 distinguished lots of music included Gibbons's Fancies of three parts 'engraved on copper': three manuscript volumes of Scarlatti cantatas: five volumes of Lalande's *Motets* (Paris, 1729): Casini's *Pensieri per l'organo*, op. 3 (Florence, 1714): an obscure work described as 'Pate's Observations on composition', and a goodly representation of Purcell and Blow. Among Shield's instruments are listed a 'viol d'amour', a 'viol di gamba', a lute and a chamber organ, which, taken with the marked bias of his music towards the seventeenth century, argue a cultivated taste for which he has hardly been given credit.

Let us now consider the really great collectors of the late eighteenth and early nineteenth century, who may be conveniently grouped together, out of strict chronological order.

The year 1814, besides its political significance, was noteworthy for the dispersal of two collections of music, exactly a century after the Britton sale —Granville Sharp's and Burney's. Sharp—the sale-catalogue spells his name with a terminal 'e'—was famous as a philanthropist and a protagonist in the struggle to abolish slavery. He was a versatile, if apparently rather unskilled performer, being equally at home on recorder, clarinet, double flute and oboe. He invented an instrument called the transverse harp. From 1775 onwards he used to give large water music-parties and receptions on his barge of forty-five tons, named the *Union Yacht*, and smaller ones on *The Apollo*, as immortalised by Zoffany. He seems to have shared his extensive library with his brothers James and William, though there is no evidence that they were active in building it up. (Some of James's music had been sold in 1792.) For at their houses, on alternate Sunday nights, Granville Sharp organised concerts of sacred music, at which he used to play the timpani.[1] Two letters in the Hardwicke Papers show that the part of his music and instruments which had come to him from Thomas Sharp, his father, had originally belonged to the composer the Hon. and Rev. Edward Finch, fifth son of the first Earl of Nottingham.

Sotheby's seem to have had some difficulty in compressing the collection into 532 lots. It included a large quantity of eighteenth-century concertos, lessons and anthems, and a good many Handel operas and oratorios. The English composers of the seventeenth century were hardly represented, and he had few madrigals, with the rather curious exception of the rare Nuremberg edition (1601) of Marenzio's five-part madrigals, which fetched the modest sum of 3s. I cannot help wondering if one of the other Sharp brothers may have been an amateur of the trumpet, for lot 349 reads: 'Trumpet concertos—a bundle—1s. 6d.' Yet by 1814 had real trumpet concertos been composed and written or printed in sufficient quantity to make up even a bundle? Sharp also owned what is the first copy of *The Bird Fancier's Delight* that I have found in any catalogue (lot 189): it fetched 6s. Another part of his collection was not sold, but given to York Minster. His bookplate, designed by himself, is charming (Pl. II*b*).[2] It shows an organ screen, across the nave of a church, surrounded by a border of three scriptural texts.

And so we pass to 'the great Dr Burney'. In any musical context, Burney is a name which evokes an admiration that tends to border on awe. In a study of collecting, the dispersal of his great library is also an invitation to pause for reflection. Not only may we consider profitably the importance and position of Burney himself as a collector, but we may also try to divine something of the philosophy that governed the private acquisition of music in general during the long era of which his library forms an apex. Note that I say 'an' apex, not 'the' apex. The position is rather curious. As an historian of music, Burney is commonly admitted to be rivalled only by

---

[1] See Prince Hoare, *Memoirs of Granville Sharp*, 2nd ed. (London, 1828), vol. I, pp. 214–16; vol. II, appendix, pp. xix, xx, xxiv; also, the article on Sharp in Brown and Stratton, *British Musical Biography* (Birmingham, 1897), and Edward Lascelles, *Granville Sharp* (London, 1928), pp. 119–26.

[2] A copy is preserved in B.M. Add. MS. 30479.

Hawkins.  But as a collector, he is tacitly assumed to be unrivalled in his own generation. This is an illusion.  He has been looked upon as a kind of solitary peak, standing apart from others and far outsoaring them in the greatness of his music library.  Seen, as it were, from the nearer slopes, he towers indeed in apparent isolation, as does the Matterhorn: but from a higher, more distant viewpoint, Burney is clearly seen to be but one of a group of five noble summits rising from adjacent ridges. The other 'peak' collectors were John Bartleman, Edward Jones, Sir John Hawkins, and Lord Fitzwilliam.

Before I discuss them in some detail, let us look back beyond the eighteenth century.  Remarkable as were the music collections of Heather, Pepys and Britton in their different ways, there seems little doubt that the *primum mobile*, the great impetus to collecting on a large scale and to the related growth of musical scholarship, came from Pepusch. Though he wrote little himself, his influence on a younger generation must have been powerful. His long direction of the Academy of Ancient Music must have made his followers aware of the inexhaustible treasures of a rich musical past that cried out for exploration.  Progress depended on the collection of manuscript and printed sources in sufficient quantity.  Even when this had been done—and it was at first a slow business—scholars and composers could only begin to understand musical history, and then translate knowledge of theory into actual performance.

From about 1720 onwards, collectors in Britain saw the horizons of musical history widening with what may often have seemed a bewildering rapidity. To Pepusch, the younger Gostling, Boyce and the brothers Hayes, to Burney and Hawkins in their youth, collecting must have become exciting in a way that later generations have never known, because of the sheer profusion of old foreign music that gradually became available. Whatever were the channels through which it reached London from the Continent— especially from Italy—there must have been intense excitement in snapping it up, in studying its relation to the rarities of early English music, and in piecing together the threads of musical history.

Burney, of course, was by far the most enterprising of the great British collectors of the Georgian era. He travelled extensively in Europe, more widely even than Lord Fitzwilliam, and brought back musical treasures copied laboriously in old libraries or ferreted out from booksellers' dark shelves in a dozen cities, notably in Venice. Even after his history was published, from 1776 to 1789, Burney seems still to have gone on collecting. For the last and in some ways the ripest fruit of his knowledge began to appear some twelve years later, in the great series of articles on musical topics which he wrote between about 1801 and 1811 and contributed anonymously to Rees's *Cyclopedia*.

That part of Burney's library which was auctioned by White in August 1814 consisted entirely of music, and amounted to 822 lots, in fourteen groups, of which the largest was 'madrigals, falas, ayres and sacred songs', amounting to 147 lots, while 'Masses and motetts' ran to seventy-seven. His huge assemblage of Italian vocal music, made into 104 lots, included thirty-one volumes of works by Perez. Handel comprised only six lots, but Haydn amounted to thirty-six. Mozart, however, though including the Breitkopf 'œuvres complettes' only made up five lots. The books on music and treatises were not auctioned, but were offered to the British Museum, where, unfortunately, they have not been kept together, and no list can now be traced. The Trustees' minutes of November 1814 show that the collection numbered 257 items, which were bought for £283. The minutes also reveal —what not even Scholes knew—that the offer originally included 'sundry curious and rare Chinese instruments', which the Trustees declined.[1]

As in history, so in collecting: Burney's name has been so habitually coupled with that of Hawkins, that we tend to forget that Burney lived on for twenty-five years after his rival's death in 1789. Yet since they began collecting at nearly the same time, I may perhaps be excused for delaying consideration of Hawkins until this point. It is a thousand pities that we do not know, and probably never shall, exactly what his music library contained, although certain categories in it are known and justly famous. So it

---

[1] P. A. Scholes, *The Great Dr Burney* (London, 1948), vol. I, p. 301, mentions the collection of instruments but not the offer of it to the British Museum.

would be unfair to relegate him to the ghost collectors to be discussed later. It must have been a pretty large collection, for without ample sources he could scarcely have written his history. Burney would never have given him free use of his collection, though Boyce, who seems to have been friendly with Hawkins, may well have opened his own treasures to the historian, as Stafford Smith certainly did. We know from Scholes that much of Hawkins's general library perished in a fire in 1785, and it may be that some of his music was burnt with it. But before this he seems to have given his noble collection of printed madrigals, motets, and the like, to George III, who added them to the royal music. In 1778 Hawkins presented his works of musical theory to the British Museum.

His son John Sidney Hawkins seems to have inherited some manuscript and printed music and certainly acquired a good deal more. The first portion was sold in 1832 by Wheatley, in 154 lots, including a number of treatises. But it was a poor sale, and rather a poor catalogue. A copy of Banister and Low's *Ayres and Dialogues* (1678), only six perfect copies of which are known in England today, fetched *6d*. The catalogue was, by the way, unusually rich in misprints, which would probably have caused no little annoyance to Sir John. For instance, Koželuch appeared as 'Korluck', and one may conjecture that the '*German Nato* [*sic*] *of English Songs*' was the well-known *German Erato*!

The second sale of the younger Hawkins's music, and the third (held not long after his death in 1842), reveal a much richer collection, including a wealth of musical theory, English, Spanish and Italian, and three volumes of manuscript anthologies of Italian music, formerly owned by Britton. These may well have once been in Sir John's possession. Even on this rather nebulous evidence, it seems likely that the elder Hawkins's collection was no mean one, though probably it could not rival the grandeur of Burney's. It is curious how shadowy a figure, at least in his musical activities, Hawkins is. His extant letters are very few and none sheds any light on his collecting.

If Burney is the Matterhorn of these towering late Georgian collectors, Hawkins, often rather surly in temper, is surely the Lyskamm. By the same token, Bartleman may be compared to the huge mass of the Breithorn, Edward Jones to the glitter of the Mischabel, and Lord Fitzwilliam to the regal elegance of Monte Rosa.

The sale of Bartleman's library occupied the auctioneer White from 20 to 27 February 1822. On the title-page of the catalogue he described it as 'a very extensive and matchless assemblage of the most choice and scarce productions and works of all the great masters, ancient and modern', and went on: 'This collection, presumed to be the finest ever brought to public sale, fully characterises the sound and superior judgement of the late possessor, in making so compleat a selection, and which as a favourite object, he accomplished by indefatigable pains and liberality.' Bartleman was a pure collector: he published or edited nothing. He was a famous bass singer, much in demand for church music, concerts and convivial gatherings. In his youth he knew Hawkins, who may have inspired his collecting zeal. It is also worth mentioning that Bartleman made an incomplete catalogue of Lord Fitzwilliam's music.

A study of the 1456 lots into which White made up Bartleman's vast collection fully bears out his high claims. In catholicity of interests and comprehensiveness Bartleman rivals Burney and in some categories surpasses him, for instance in the 238 lots comprising 'masses, motetts, madrigals, etc.' There are also 245 lots of Italian operas and songs, and over 150 lots of treatises and theoretical works. A nice association-piece is a J. C. Smith manuscript of some Handel anthems presented by George III to Aylward. There are numerous items of such rarity as Robinson's *Schoole of Musick for the Lute*, Bathe's *Brief Introduction to the Skill of Song*, two of the Sadeler single-sheet prints of motets by Verdonck which, dating respectively from 1584 and 1585, are the earliest known engraved musical compositions.[1] Only one copy is now known of the work described as 'Perkins's Mysterys of the Violoncello' and the manuscript 'Deed of the Academy Foundation, 1719' (lot 1409) seems quite to have vanished. Even with the

---

[1] The music printed from engraved plates in p. 71 and p. 78 of Vincenzo Galilei's *Dialogo della musica antiqua e della moderna* (Florence, 1581), consists only of tables of certain notes in the modes.

advantage of such sales as Gostling and Burney to draw on, Bartleman's collection was a staggering achievement, for each of these 1456 lots contained an average of five items. It stands as by far the largest until the time of Ouseley, Marshall and Cummings.

While Bartleman published nothing, Edward Jones, on the other hand, the Welsh composer who enjoyed the proud title of 'Bard to the King', did publish several anthologies of old music. But even so, had the sale-catalogues of his collections not survived, these anthologies would have given no clue to the range of his musical interests. There were three sales of Jones's collections. His vast general library, which shows him to have been a man of very wide culture, was auctioned in 1823, and the first part of his music library in 1824, two months before his death. The second part of his music was sold in 1825. The total number of lots in the two music sales, which also included some books on non-musical subjects, was about 550. Though not nearly as large as Bartleman's, this collection was superior to it in the high proportion and superb quality of the publications from the late sixteenth and early seventeenth centuries. Many of the choicest pieces ultimately passed to Rimbault.

Some of them were originally bought by a dealer named Thorpe (presumably Thomas Thorpe), at prices which, even allowing for relative money values, are remarkable: *Parthenia Inviolata*, 12s.; *Ornithoparcus* (1609), 1s. 6d.; Dowland's *First Booke of Ayres*, lacking two leaves, 7s. 6d.; Dowland's *Lachrimae*, 14s.; Leighton's *Teares*, 17s.; the flute and violin parts of Morley's *Consort Lessons* (1611), 1s.; Rosseter's *Consort Lessons* (1609), 1s.; Morley's *Plaine and easie Introduction*, 6s.; a contemporary manuscript of Coperario's *Fantasias of 3 parts*, 1s.; the complete programmes of the 'Musical Society at the Nag's Head, Leadenhall Street, 1770–1778', 18s.

Other prices were relatively high. Longman paid £5. 2s. 6d. for Le Roy's *Briefe and Plaine Instruction* (1574); £2 for Amerbach's *Orgel- oder Tabulaturbuch*, 1571 (presumably Cramer's copy), owned by J. S. Bach and Burney; £5. 5s. for *Pammelia* (1609). Two other choice items were Hudgebut's *Vade mecum for the Lovers of musick, shewing the excellency of the Rechorder* [sic]

(1679), now known in only one copy; and Dean's *Compleat Tutor for the Violin* (1707), of which no copy can be traced. Two curiosities may be noticed, described in the catalogue thus: 'Perkins's Fancies. Trios in imitation of various birds and beasts. 3 vol. MS' (was this, one wonders, written by the same Perkins who composed *Mysterys of the Violoncello* ?), and 'Turkish and Greek music from the library of Sir John Hawkins, 1796, 97'. Such were a few of the treasures owned by Edward Jones, who brought music-collecting to a new peak of excellence at the end of the Georgian era.

The only one of the really great music collections of the later eighteenth century that went on growing in the early nineteenth century and then survived intact was that of Richard Fitzwilliam, seventh Viscount Fitzwilliam of Meryon (1745–1816). The extent and splendour of Lord Fitzwilliam's music are well known from the published catalogue, but something must be said of his character as a collector. Early in life he received musical instruction from competent composers and continued his studies into the seventeen-nineties. In 1764 he owned a harpsichord which was kept in Thomas Gray's rooms at Peterhouse.[1] Lord Fitzwilliam was therefore fully able to appreciate the significance of all that he acquired, both during his extensive travels in France and Italy, and in England. His tidy habit of noting place and date upon his purchases sheds some light on sources (Pl. I*b*). He also purchased from the libraries of such notable collectors as Boyce and Bever.

In Lord Fitzwilliam's collection, Italian music bulks large, but his taste was wide enough to acquire French music by such then unfashionable composers as Lalande, Lully and Rameau. We know that Lord Fitzwilliam was given the Virginal Book by Bremner, but it remains a complete mystery how he acquired the mass of fragments and sketches in Handel's autograph, now bound in twelve volumes in a nineteenth-century binding. We can infer from his influential association with the great Festival of 1784 that Handel attracted him strongly. He may have known the younger Smith before about 1774 when the latter still possessed all the Handel autographs.

[1] R. W. Ketton-Cremer, *Thomas Gray* (Cambridge, 1955), p. 205.

But this is pure surmise. Lord Fitzwilliam had very wide contacts and was clearly always eager to make his library of music as distinguished and extensive as possible, and herein lies his outstanding quality as a collector.

After the splendours of music-collecting in the later Georgian period, the pageant of the next seventy years begins on an altogether lower plane. In the number and quality of collectors active up to the early eighteen-forties it is pitched, as it were, in a minor key, and the tonal background shifts from a ringing *maestoso* in D major to the quietness of the sub-dominant.

The two collectors whose music comes first to notice were men of very different character. Thomas Greatorex, whose library was sold by T. H. Watson in 360 lots in 1832, was born near Chesterfield in 1758. His successful career as organist, conductor, mathematician, astronomer and natural historian was furthered in his youth through the interest of the Earl of Sandwich. Between 1786 and 1788 he travelled widely abroad, and when in Rome was introduced to the Young Pretender, Charles Edward Stuart, 'with whom' as Husk says in *Grove*, 'he so ingratiated himself as to induce the Prince to bequeath to him a large quantity of valuable manuscript music'. This fact is also mentioned on the title-page of the sale-catalogue. The Pretender's interest in collecting music seems quite unknown to his biographers. The most important of the items so identified was seven volumes of a collection of ninety cantatas by Alessandro Scarlatti. (The Prince's copy of a manuscript of Feo's *Andromacca*, later owned by Greatorex, Gauntlett and Oliphant, is now B.M. Add. MS. 24303.) While Greatorex also possessed such choice pieces as Peri's *Euridice* of 1600 and some early editions of Palestrina, all these are overshadowed by lot 252, the so-called 'Handel Bookcase', which contained the famous collection of sixty-seven volumes of J. C. Smith copies of Handel (later known as the 'Lennard Collection' and now in the Fitzwilliam Museum). It was acquired at the sale by John Ireland, Dean of Westminster, for 115 guineas. This is, I think, a hitherto unknown provenance for this famous set of Handel manuscripts; it is mentioned in the account of the Greatorex sale given by *The Harmonicon*,[1]

---

[1] Vol. x (1832), p. 118.

which remarked incidentally: 'The music as a whole produced fair prices, considering the state of the country.' It is perhaps worth mentioning that Greatorex had acquired a good deal of his less important music at the Sydney sale of 1813.

William Kitchiner, the son of a wealthy coal merchant, went to Eton, and later took medical degrees, but never practised. He composed a good deal of music and wrote some books about it. He sold part of his library as early as 1809, when he was only thirty-two. He died suddenly in 1827, 'regular and abstemious in his habits', says Husk, 'but while practising the precepts he gave to others, he was unable to prolong his own life beyond the age of 50'. Sotheby sold the residue of his music in 1838, and perpetrated such vague descriptions as lot 190 'MSS scores of Haydn, in the autograph of the composer, very interesting'—purchased by Purday for 7s. The rarities included the now lost virginal manuscript which included Bull's 'God save the King'. Kitchiner also owned the notable collection of eighteenth-century English songs, once Burney's, and containing an index in his hand. It is now in the British Museum. Sotheby noted the fact that 'this collection of music is for the most part uniformly bound in russia, by Kalthoeber'—the only mention of a binder's name I have found in any auction catalogue of music until much later in the nineteenth century. Kitchiner's second sale was one of the earliest in which Rimbault's name appears as a buyer.

In the mid eighteen-thirties there comes to notice Charles Britiffe Smith, who is the earliest known collector of autograph letters of musicians. On 26 June 1835[1] he wrote to Dawson Turner offering his collection for £50, and stated that it comprised '290 letters and autographs accompanied by portraits of the writers where I have been able to obtain them'. The composers included Arne, Beethoven, Boyce, Cherubini, Handel, Haydn and Rossini. Whether or not Turner accepted Smith's offer is not certain: at any rate a remarkably similar collection of letters appeared in an Evans sale on 27 May 1842.

The name of William Young Ottley deserves mention because at the sale

---

[1] See A. N. L. Munby, *The Cult of the Autograph Letter* (London, 1962), pp. 66, 67.

of his music in 1838 lot 28 comprised the so-called 'Dublin' score of *Messiah*, which was purchased for £1. 1s. by one Warner, who may have been an agent acting for another branch of the family. For this manuscript later passed to Captain Edward J. Ottley, who presented it to Sir Frederick Ouseley in May 1867. In March of this same year, Captain Ottley likewise presented to Ouseley an early manuscript of *Acis and Galatea*, which also seems to have come from the sale of 1838. William Ottley apparently lived for some time in Italy, for his small collection was mostly Italian. In Rome he patronised two composers named Persichini and Lorenzini: lot 48 consisted of the latter's 'Burlesque Lamentation for the departure of Mr Ottley from Rome'.

In the early years of Victoria's reign, the number of collectors known from auctions begins to multiply so much that I can only mention those who are of general importance, or possessed some items of outstanding interest. But before we consider collectors, let us pause at the curious affair of the Shipton hoard. In the issue of the *Musical World* for 27 August 1840 there appeared a long letter, headed 'Discovery of a Collection of Ancient English Music'. It reads as follows:

To the Editor of the Musical World.

DISCOVERY OF A COLLECTION OF ANCIENT ENGLISH MUSIC.

Sir,—In an old family mansion at Shipton, near Woodstock, there has been lately found by the present proprietor, on opening the ground to make some repairs to the house, four large iron chests filled with music-books and other documents, consisting of treatises, masses, motetts, madrigals, &c., by all the English composers and writers from the year 1480 down to the year 1649, as well as foreign publications of a similar kind and of the same period, both printed and in manuscript. The place in which these iron chests were found was a large and dry stone cellar or vault, underground, the entrance to which appeared originally to have been in a recess in the wall (blocked up) from one of the lower apartments or cellars, perhaps managed by a spring, of which there appear some remains on the door. The whole of the books appear to be in their original bindings, some in wooden covers with clasps, others in old stout leathern bindings and tied with silken strings, and others in old vellum: they are all perfect and in fine condition.

Being permitted, at the intercession of a friend, to see the collection, I managed to take nearly a complete list of the whole; this occupied me nearly two days. Of this list I send you a brief sketch:-

Copies of "Ravenscroft's Pamelia, 1600". "Deuteromelia, 1609". "Melismata, 1610". "Brief Discourse, 1614" and another work by the same author, not known. "Musalia, or Pleasant Diversions in Rime, several varieties of catches, roundels, canons, freemen's songs, madrigals, balletas, fancies, gleemen's songs, and countrie dances, fitting for all sorts of humoures, by Thomas Ravenscroft, B.M., imprinted at London, and are to be had at the sign of the Bible and Musicke-booke, neare St. Mildred's Church in ye Poultrie, at Nicholas Freeman, his house, 4to, 1613". This volume contains abundance of matter for the ballad and song collector; it has near three hundred pages of music. "Youthe's Recreation, or the Dancing-master, with directions; the first of the kind printed in England, containing thirty new countrie dances: London, printed for John Playford at his shop in ye Strand, oblong, 4to, 1648". A very thin volume, not above twenty pages, "Parthenia, or Musicke's Maidenhead for the Virginals, being the first musicke ever printed of the kinde, by Doctor John Bull, William Birde, and Orlando Gibbons, gentlemen of her Majesty's chappell: imprinted at London by Peter Short, dwelling on Bread-street-hill, at the signe of the Starre, folio, 1600; dedicated to Queen Elizabeth." "Severall Interludes, with the music at the end, printed by Wynkin de Worde and Richard Pynson, particularly the 'Four Elements' by Rastall, 1519". This is truly the most astonishing collection ever heard of: it contains complete sets of the madrigals and part-songs by Morley, Bird, Tallis, Mundy, Warde, Weelkes, Dowland, Wilbye, Helton [*sic*], Alison, Conkine [*sic*], East, Tomkins, Amner, Lichfild, Porter, Pilkington, Bennett, Croce, Kirbye, Farmer, Gibbons, Younge, Watson, Leighton, Bull, Firabosco [*sic*], Bateson, Melton, &c. &c., Luca Marenzio's nine sets of madrigals to five voices (Englished) unknown; six sets to six voices; ditto four sets to four voices; three ditto ditto; villanellas by ditto, two sets; transalpinos, four sets; and apparently every madrigal and part song as well as concert lessons &c., ever printed in England, some as early as 1560: and among others the following extraordinary set, "Songs to Sondry Natures to three and fowere voyces, set by W. Cornyshe, Maiester Taverner, Dr. Robert Fayrfax, Pygott, Ashwell, R. Jones, J. Gwynnethe and Dr. Copere: imprinted at London by Richard Pynson, dwelling in Fleete streete, M.D.,XXX. (according to the Colophon)."

There is an immense quantity of continental publications from 1480 down to 1641, consisting of masses, motetts, madrigalls, chansons, by all the masters of those times in Italy and the Netherlands. Also a rare collection of early treatises by Zinctor [*sic*], Anselems, Gaffurie, Zartino [*sic*], Zacchrie [*sic*], Galelei [*sic*], &c. Some very early scores of masses, motetts, and madrigals, particularly one "Cypriano de Rores, motetts in four and five voci en partitura: impressa a Venetia par a Gardane, 1560, folio 24; staved paper, 432 pages."

A number of Dutch ballad or song-books printed at Antwerp, Amsterdam, and Haerlem, containing national tunes of all countries.

There is also a large quantity of English church music in MS. &c. and seven large vellum MSS., consisting of very old songs in parts on opposite sides, to English words, and in black and red notes intermixed.

The present proprietor does not know what to do with the books and is very anxious to make money of them. I advised him to offer them to the British Museum or the Gresham Library at a certain price for the whole; but he does not appear to like that trouble, and says if he has not an offer personally, by private contract, he will call in an auctioneer, and sell them on the premises.

The following copy of a very curious historical document fell from out of one of the books; it fully explains the reason why these chests of books were concealed. It was during the civil wars previous to the death of Charles the First, when so much devastation was committed throughout England, and everything in the shape of musical service books as well as other things were destroyed by the parliament army.

"To Brown, Clerii, Parliamentorum:

"These are to will, require and command you, and every of you, to forbear, under any pretence whatsoever, to prejudice or offer any damage to the University of Oxford, or to any of the schools, colleges, halls, libraries, chappells, or other places belonging to the said university by plundering the same or any part thereof in any kind whatsoever. Hereof fail not as you will answer the contrary at your perils. Given under my hand and seal the 7th day of March, 1642. (Signed) "ESSEX".

"To all colonels, lieutenant-colonels, captains and all other officers soldiers of the army under my command."

The above was a copy probably sent as a warning to [the] then possessor to place his most valuable effects in some secure place.

I am, sir, your's &c.

A MEMBER OF THE PURCELL CLUB

Aug. 24th, 1840.

This member of the Purcell Club[1] had a nice sense of history, period and topography, and an awareness of the possibilities of imprint. He conjures up two 'pre-firsts' (*Parthenia* and *The Dancing Master*), an unknown work of Ravenscroft[2] and a complete set of the parts of the *XX sōges*, dated 1530, with Pynson's imprint. (It is a little odd that Pynson's will was proved in

---

[1] Founded 1836, dissolved 1863. No list of the members, limited to forty-two, seems to be extant. See Grove, 1st edn.

[2] Apparently taken seriously by Pulver in his *Biographical Dictionary of Old English Music* (London, 1927), p. 407.

February 1530, which suggests that he died in 1529.) The writer of the letter must have been acquainted with the then owner, at present unknown, of the bassus part of the *XX sōges*, the only one surviving of the edition which was for long (and still is sometimes) incorrectly ascribed to de Worde. He was, of course, unaware of the fragments of two other parts, in Westminster Abbey Library, which reveal the imprint 'at the signe of the Black Morens'.[1] 'Brown, clerii [*sic*] Parliamentorum' was possibly intended to be Sir Richard Browne, the well-known Parliamentary general, who had the task of reducing the Oxford district in 1644. There still is an old manor house at Shipton, with cellars very similar to those mentioned.[2]

The thing is, of course, a hoax, and I mention it as the only musical one that appears to be known. But who was the writer of the letter? Was it Warren, Rimbault or Edward Taylor (the President of the Purcell Club)? Why so elaborately, to deceive so few? Is it just possible that it was inspired by the 'sale' of the fifty-two unique—but non-existent—early books in Comte de Fortsas's library, advertised in Belgium for 10 August 1840? Or is a bare fortnight too short an interval between this hoax and the appearance of the letter, dated 24 August, in the issue of the *Musical World* that appeared on 27 August? But, remember, this was then a weekly publication.

We may now return from fantasy to fact, to the partly known fame of the library collected by the Rev. Christian Ignatius Latrobe, friend of Haydn, editor of hymn tunes and of early Italian and German sacred music. He died in 1836, but his music was not dispersed until 2 May 1842, when it was auctioned by T. Fletcher. The only known copy of the catalogue is in the Harding Collection. The sale was summarised by the *Musical World*, which also gave some prices. Latrobe seems to have specialised in English church music and in Italian masses, motets and madrigals, partly derived from Gostling and Bever. Among the purchasers were Oliphant, Chappell, Hullah, Rimbault and Warren. It seems that other music besides Latrobe's appeared at this

[1] See H. M. Nixon, 'The Book of XX Songs', *The British Museum Quarterly*, vol. XVI, no. 2 (1951), pp. 33–5.
[2] When I inspected them in 1953, with Mr (now Professor) Thurston Dart, they were mostly bricked up.

sale, for the *Musical World* said it was 'partly' his and went on: 'and we are given to understand, a greater portion, the collection of Mr Cooper'.[1]

All the available details concerning the sad story of John Stafford Smith's great collection comprising 2191 volumes (of which but a fraction was used for his *Musica Antiqua* of 1812) are given in Husk's article on him in Grove. At Smith's death in 1836, his music passed to his daughter, who became insane, so that her property had to be sold to maintain her. The anonymous catalogue made for the sale of 24 April 1844 by an ignorant auctioneer[2] contained such descriptions as 'Fifty books, various' and such books as were described at all were catalogued from the backs. The collection was thus dispersed almost without trace. A small part of it was acquired, presumably at auction, by the firm of Hamilton & Bird (later C. Hamilton) of Islington; no. 10 of their catalogues for 1844[3] lists 113 items, printed and manuscript, formerly in Smith's possession. These include the Mulliner Book (£6. 6s.: see Pl. VII), Diruta's *Il Transilvano* (£1. 5s.) and the copy of the *Ulm Gesangbuch* (1538) formerly owned by J. S. Bach and C. P. E. Bach, presented by the latter to Smith at Hamburg in 1772, acquired later by Havergal, and now in the Euing Library. Another small part of Smith's music seems to have remained in the stock of Calkin & Budd, and was sold with other collections at two sales in 1852 and 1853. As usual, Oliphant secured some odd parts of madrigals. One curious item (possibly lot 20 in the Callcott sale) was a work by Princess Elizabeth, daughter of George III: 'Cock Robin set to music: privately printed for distribution among members of the Royal Family'; it survives in a copy owned by D. Richardson of Charles River, Massachusetts.

The great double-bass player, Dragonetti, who settled in London in 1794, and died there in 1846, was an inveterate collector of many things besides music—pictures, engravings, dolls, snuff-boxes and instruments. His musical library was never sold *in toto*: he gave a good many manuscripts to Vincent Novello, and a number of them appear in the sale of the latter's

---

[1] The older of two musicians of this name, who were both assistant organists at St Paul's: see p. 51.

[2] Not now identifiable, as no copy can be found: presumably Husk (see *Grove*) had seen one.

[3] Copy in a private collection.

library, in 1852. Novello later gave some volumes to the Fitzwilliam Museum and others to the British Museum, and Ouseley acquired a few more which are now at Tenbury. But the bulk of his collections, to the extent of over 180 volumes of operatic scores by composers from Alessandro Scarlatti onwards, Dragonetti himself bequeathed to the British Museum.[1]

In 1846 Thomas Mackinlay printed for private circulation *A Catalogue of original Letters and Manuscripts in the Autograph of distinguished Musicians, Composers, Performers and Vocalists*. It is the only thing of its kind published during the nineteenth century, and the richness of the collection reflects great credit on the judgement and enterprise of Mackinlay, who was at one time a partner in the firm of Goulding, D'Almaine & Co. His collection, which also included autograph music and portraits of musicians, was sold in 1866. Some of the letters later found their way into the collection of Andrew G. Kurtz, and have passed into the British Museum as part of Add. MS. 33965.

Three collections of music were amassed by noblemen during this era: the first to be auctioned was that of the Duke of Sussex, entrusted to Christie in 1846. (The libraries of the Duke of Cambridge and the Earl of Falmouth will come into my third lecture.) The 210 lots of the Duke of Sussex's music reveal a rather pedestrian taste. The total fetched was only £36. 7s., after which sum the auctioneer's clerk added three derisory exclamation marks. The highest price, £2. 10s. was paid for the Cianchettini & Sperati edition of symphonies by Haydn, Mozart and Beethoven. The library of one Louis Gantter,[2] together with his instruments, was sold in August 1846. It is noteworthy for the fact that it is the first collection of music ever sold by Puttick & Simpson, who, from this year onwards, quickly dominated the auctions of music. James Fell Puttick (*c.* 1821–73), who has been described as 'a man of wide musical connexions and interests' must have been the

---

[1] Now Add. MSS. 15979–16160, and including one large volume of keyboard music. A full list is in *Additions to the Manuscripts of the British Museum, 1846–1847* (London, 1864), pp. 147–53.

[2] Perhaps he was the same as the Mr Gantter who gave a series of lectures on ecclesiastical music in 1846, with the help of 'a chorus selected from the choirs of Westminster Abbey, St Paul's and the Temple'. See Scholes, *The Mirror of Music* (London, 1947), p. 71.

driving force in their success.[1] Another reason undoubtedly lay in their special knowledge of the musical instruments which formed, now as in the eighteenth century, such an attractive and historically valuable portion of so many libraries. Henceforth until after 1900, I shall only mention the auctioneer if he was other than Puttick.

In 1847 Sotheby disposed of the collection of Enoch Hawkins, of the Chapel Royal, St James's and Vicar Choral of Westminster Abbey. Lot 133 was optimistically described as the original manuscript of *Acis and Galatea*. The buyers knew better, for this copy only fetched £1. 12s. (It is in this sale that we meet again (cf. p. 28) the delightful word 'airiettes', used to describe some songs by Haydn. Whether due to a misprint or a cataloguer's flight of fancy, this is surely a most desirable addition to the vocabulary of musical description!) This Hawkins was, by the way, no relation of Sir John's son, John Sidney, whose notable collection was, as I mentioned earlier, sold in three parts, in 1832 and 1843.

The collection of Lady Mary Sykes, auctioned in 1847, was of a remarkably wide scope, for it ranged from Byrd's *Psalmes, Sonets and Songs of Sadnes* (1588) to operas of the eighteenth and early nineteenth centuries. A section of organ music included (lot 133) 'Bach's grand studies for the Organ, 8 books in 1 volume, arranged with separate violoncello or double bass part by Dragonetti'. Lady Sykes also had a number of odd parts of English madrigals, which were bought cheap by Thomas Oliphant. This is the first time his name appears in a priced catalogue as a buyer of these items.

Henry John Gauntlett was a solicitor who became a famous organist, and gained more repute from his psalters and hymnals than from his compositions. He sold his library in 1847 when he was only forty-two, and lived until 1876. The catalogue is elaborately grouped both by classes and by composers, the latter ranging from Bach to Mendelssohn. Some exceedingly rare early theory included Diruta's *Il Transilvano*, Gafori's *Practica musicae* of 1512 and Pepusch's copy, from the Heber collection, of Salinas's *De musica libri septem*. His taste for early organ music is seen in a large

---

[1] A. N. L. Munby, *Phillipps Studies*, vol. IV (Cambridge, 1956), p. 10.

manuscript containing Italian organ works of the mid sixteenth century and another of English works dated from about 1550 to 1650. He typifies the unsuspected musical catholicity of the lesser Victorians.

If the name of Johann Andreas Stumpff is remembered at all today, it is probably because of the visit he paid to Beethoven in 1818, and of which he left some account. Stumpff, a harp-maker from Ruhla in Thuringia who settled in London, had acquired—probably from J. A. André in 1814 (and not, as he himself stated, from Mozart's widow in 1811)—one of the best collections of Mozart autographs ever owned privately in England. He likewise possessed nine autographs of Beethoven, and others by Spohr and Cipriani Potter. The sentimental part of Stumpff's collection included 'the initials of Mozart and his wife, worked in their own hair'; 'a small quantity of the hair of Goethe'; and 'a chased silver snuff box, with a lock of Beethoven's hair set in a locket outside, and original verses[1] by A. J. Stumpff engraved within'. At the sale of his effects in 1847, this snuff-box fetched £7. 7s., twice as much as the autograph of any one of the ten great Mozart quartets! When it reappeared at Sotheby's in 1960 (14 January, lot 88), it fetched £56.

It is a great pity that Ignaz Moscheles's library was inextricably mixed up with other properties at a sale in 1847 which was distinguished by some rare part-books and instrumental works of the seventeenth century. The instruments included a theorbo-lute by 'Laux-Maller [i.e. Maler, d. 1552], from the Duke of Chandos, Cannons', the only mention I have found of any musical item from this establishment. It was bought by Ayrton for £1. 2s.

To Timothy Essex, a secondary composer born in 1764, fell the unusual distinction of living long enough to acquire early Purcell editions, much

---

[1] The verses read:

> True friendship will with friendship share
>  All that it values most.
> Accept this pledge—Beethoven's hair
>  Is on its lid embossed.
>
> When you, dear Mey'r, a pinch shall take
>  Your spirits to restore,
> Then may this box old friendship wake
>  When Stumpff is e'en no more.

music published in the seventeen-thirties and seventeen-forties, and first editions of Balfe, Bishop and Mendelssohn. His large library was sold in 1848 in 394 lots, in which, rather remarkably, the only non-musical item was 'Rouss's'[1] translation of Silius Italicus! A few of the early eighteenth-century works had been owned by Philip Hayes. Smaller, but much more distinguished, was the collection of the Rev. Samuel Picart, Rector of Hartlebury and Prebendary of Hereford, who seems to have been interested in almost everything from Dowland to Paganini. He owned a small but choice group of J. S. Bach—still an unusual taste for the eighteen-forties in England—including apparently early manuscript copies and 'Two trios, for 2 violins and bass, in score, MS, believed to be autograph'. But his finest piece was undoubtedly lot 207, 'A curious virginal Book, containing compositions of Bird, Holborne, Lodwick, Pilkington, Cuttinge, Dowland, Ferebosco [*sic*], Alfonso, Valentine. This volume would appear to have been formerly in the possession of Queen Mary and Phillip [*sic*] of Spain, whose arms are impressed on the sides'. (The book, still resplendent in its original binding, is now in the British Museum, Add. MS. 31392, but the arms are not those of Queen Mary and King Philip.) Paganini's twenty-four caprices, with an unpublished accompaniment by J. L. Hatton, fetched twelve guineas. The last music collection to be noticed from the eighteen-forties was that of Sir Giffin Wilson, who not only possessed James Kent's copy of Morley's *Introduction* but also specialised in harp music, which was made up into six large lots. An Erard harp was among his instruments. I have found no other collector with a similarly pronounced interest.

The mid nineteenth century is a convenient point at which to pause and take stock. After the prodigious wave of collecting which overflowed from the late eighteenth century into the first three decades of the nineteenth, the swollen stream naturally lost some of its momentum. But beneath the apparently sluggish surface fresh currents were being formed which, after the brief slackening during the eighteen-thirties and early eighteen-forties, were soon to surge up again and spread more widely and strongly than ever before.

---

[1] Presumably that by Thomas Ross, Keeper of the Royal Libraries, first published in 1661.

# LECTURE III

# THE VICTORIANS OF THE GOLDEN
# AGE: 1850 TO 1899

We may open the eighteen-fifties by considering two aristocratic collectors, the Duke of Cambridge and the Earl of Falmouth, whose libraries were dispersed in 1850 and 1853 respectively. The Duke seems to have had a special liking for violin duets, of which he had a great quantity, notably from the early years of the century. But Purcell also had his place, no less than Handel. The large-paper copy of Arnold's edition was bought by Lord Falmouth for £19. 19s. Something of a curiosity is a copy of Mainzer's famous *Gaelic Psalm Tunes*, in a tartan silk binding. That the Duke of Cambridge was a methodical collector is shown by the fact that he kept a catalogue, with *incipits*, of all his instrumental music. This was sold as lot 250, on which Puttick's cataloguer remarked: 'this, being a *catalogue thématique*, is valuable for any library'.

Lord Falmouth owned a very large library which included a remarkably varied selection of printed music, from Simpson's *Chelys* of 1667 onwards. Concertos by Avison and Tessarini, a good deal of J. S. Bach, twenty volumes of Walsh editions of Handel, lead on to galops by Labitzky. His notable collection of musical portraits, comprising eighty-seven lots, was derived from T. M. Alsager. There were also three volumes of Whistling's *Handbuch* and a large parcel of catalogues, which may be taken to suggest a certain bibliographical turn of mind. But his choicest item was surely the autograph of Haydn's *Armida*.[1] A very fine and varied collection of old instruments reflected the Earl's active practical interest in music.

John Scott, a doctor resident in Bedford Square, London, whose small collection was sold in 1850, had some rare early pieces, one part (unspecified)

[1] Now R.C.M. MS. 276.

of Morley's *Consort Lessons* (1611) and Morley's *Introduction*, bought respectively by Lonsdale and Cummings, two names we shall meet later. Prices were mostly very low: Galilei's *Dialogo* of 1602 fetched but 2*s*. In J. P. Street's sale of 1851, the choicest items were not such as might perhaps have been expected of a collector who was librarian of the Madrigal Society. Though he did own some now exceedingly rare sets of early Dutch and Italian motets, he had few madrigals. But his small Purcell collection was outstanding. Some good manuscripts owned by Street are now in the library of Gresham College.

Here we may note the sale (comparable in its unusual delay to four others, all of the eighteen-seventies; see below, p. 59) of a famous eighteenth-century collection. It was in 1740 that the poet Thomas Gray, then residing in Florence, had begun to accumulate the remarkable assemblage of Italian music, mostly operatic airs in score, which was one of his great treasures. Gray added to it after his return to England, and had it handsomely bound in vellum, in ten volumes. These were sold by Sotheby in August 1851, and were purchased by Hamilton for £12. They reappeared in 1886 in the library of an American collector, Charles W. Frederickson, and their subsequent history has been outlined by Henry Krehbiel,[1] who also describes the music in some detail. Nine of these volumes are now in the library of W. S. Lewis at Farmington, Connecticut.

Many madrigals and some fine motets are to be found in Vincent Novello's collection, which was sold in two parts, the first in 1852, and the second in September 1862, nearly a year after his death. Oliphant secured some good bargains at the 1852 sale; it seems pretty clear that the taste for Italian music of the later sixteenth and early seventeenth century was limited. The sixth book of Marenzio's 5-voice madrigals complete (1595) made only 23*s*. Novello's interest did not lie only in vocal and sacred music. He had such diverse instrumental works as Vitali's *Balletti, corrente alla francese* (1682), the autograph of Samuel Wesley's trio for three pianos, and a manu-

---

[1] *Music and Manners of the Classical Period* (New York, 1898), pp. 3–39, 'Gray's Musical Collection'. Here the volumes are stated to be bound in 'hogskin'. The 1851 sale-catalogue says 'vellum'.

script score of the 'Microcosm Concerto'[1] attributed to Handel (lot 106, 1852). The 1862 sale included the proofs of an edition of Mendelssohn's *Six grand Organ Concertos*, with the composer's corrections, which went to that discerning collector Lonsdale for 9s. 6d. Novello's taste also ran to such rarities as Ammonius's *Libri tres odarum ecclesiasticarum* (1579 edition). Altogether, he was as great a collector of old music as an editor of it.

Novello's large collection was in many respects characteristic of others built up by Victorian scholars, teachers and performers: it served both for research and daily use. Why were these large personal libraries needed? One reason was the utter lack of adequate library resources elsewhere. Even after the passing of the Public Libraries Act in 1850, it was many years before they contained much music. It was much the same in the University Libraries. Even the music collections of the British Museum offered little help to researchers, because its catalogues fell far short of what was needed. As early as 1824[2] Novello had realised this deficiency. He put forward a very sensible plan to strengthen the Museum's collection of music, and improve its availability, under his own direction. But nothing came of it. Oliphant built up the printed collections in the eighteen-forties, and published a summary catalogue of the music manuscripts in 1842. But scholars had to wait for improvement in the catalogues until Hughes-Hughes and Squire began their labours in 1882 and 1885 respectively. Meanwhile, the editors, the singers, the professors and the composers amassed their own exemplars of rare early music, and laboriously copied by hand their material for performance and study, working far longer hours at home than they could have done in the British Museum, at least in the winter months up to 1879.[3]

There was an unusual little sale in June 1853 which brings to notice two

[1] The 'Microcosm' seems to have been a musical clock: see Scholes, *Oxford Companion to Music*, 9th edition (1955), p. 621: and William C. Smith, *Handel. A descriptive Catalogue of the early Editions* (London, 1960), p. 275.

[2] See A. Hyatt King, 'The Music Room of the British Museum, 1753–1953', in *Proceedings of the Royal Musical Association*, session 79 (1952/3), pp. 66, 67.

[3] The electric light was introduced in the Reading Room in March 1879, when 'Jablochoff candles' were tried. They proved unreliable: see *The British Museum Reading Room, 1857–1957. Centenary Exhibition* [Catalogue]. *May–June 1957*, p. 15.

diverse collectors—first the Rev. George Butler, Dean of Peterborough (who had nearly all his music bound in 'russia extra, gilt', whether *The Ladies Collection of Glees* or Crotch's *Specimens*) and, second, Dr John Stokoe, who had been medical attendant upon Napoleon at St Helena. Dr Stokoe collected a curious range in chamber music, from Corelli through the eighteenth century to Beethoven and Kreutzer, with which he presumably whiled away the hours of his isolation in the South Atlantic. I mention Dr Stokoe as an instance of a collector who gains greatly in interest through an unusual association.

When Richard Clark's library was sold in two sales, three years before his death in 1856, one of them contained no fewer than 222 copies, divided into three lots, of his own book *Reminiscences of Handel*. Perhaps Clark was not taken very seriously as a writer even in his lifetime! His history of 'God save the King' shows him as a muddled dilettante, and such too is his character as a collector. He was the proud possessor of an unusual item (lot 528 in the sale of 28 June 1853), described as 'The Anvil and Hammer of Thomas Powell with which he beat the accompaniment to the air sung by the Blacksmith in the hearing of Handel'. Clark did, however, own some rare music, including Gamble's scarce *Airs and Dialogues*, and he had a copy of *Les Pseaumes de David* (1562) by Marot and Bèze, bound in fish-skin, gilt, and (said Puttick's cataloguer) 'unmentioned by Brunet: nor in the collections of Heber, the Duke of Sussex, or Mr G. Cooper'.[1] No copy appears in the Sussex sale of 1846, which was undistinguished, but the Duke may have had some rare, old books not sold at that time. The third Clark sale, of 1857, is less important.

Those who think of Sir Henry Rowley Bishop as the composer of 'Home, sweet home' and as the dastardly adapter of operas by Mozart and others, should reflect that he was also Professor of Music successively at Edinburgh and Oxford. His collection of music, sold soon after his death in 1855, reveals both the practical and the scholarly side of his musicianship. Over

---

[1] Possibly George Cooper, Assistant Organist of St Paul's, whose music library was sold on 9 December 1844. See p. 43.

fifty lots in the sale-catalogue are specifically stated to comprise music used by Bishop in his lectures and in his glee performances. They include some quite rare items by Gluck, Lully and Grétry. He also owned such un-expected books as Simpson's *Compendium* (1667), an early edition of Ptolemy's *Harmonicorum Libri III*, treatises by Marpurg and Mace. The width of his musical sympathies is shown by manuscripts of choruses from Henry Lawes and of selections from Purcell. It is probably not generally known that Bishop wrote additional accompaniments to Arne's *Artaxerxes*. This is, perhaps, more in line with his adaptations of *Sonnambula* and *Robert le Diable*, the autographs of both being found in his library. Bishop the collector sheds some new light on Bishop the musician.

William Ayrton is probably best remembered today as a founder-member of the Philharmonic Society, as editor of *The Harmonicon*, and as compiler of the eight-volume anthology, the *Musical Library*, first published in 1834. His musical tastes were far wider than even these activities might indicate. His collection was sold in 1858, in 478 lots, and reveals a notable range of interests and considerable pertinacity. There were thirty-one lots of a very large quantity of opera libretti from 1629 onwards, French, Italian and English; eleven lots of musical portraits, one lot alone comprising 295; a volume containing Peri's *Euridice* and Caccini's *Nuove musiche* rubbed shoulders with the autograph of Mozart's clarinet trio, the latter not known by Köchel-Einstein ever to have been in England. (It fetched, by the way, £3. 3*s*.) Ayrton also owned a copy of Purcell's *The Prophetess* presented by the composer to James Talbot, presumably the author of the now famous notes for a treatise on instruments, Christ Church MS. 1187. Much of his large general collection is clearly related to the publication of the *Musical Library*, but there is a good deal else that bespeaks both a fine antiquarian taste and a flair for the unusual in his own times. A Trieste edition of *Il Crociato*, with many remarks in Meyerbeer's hand, makes a strong contrast to autographs of Locke and Haydn. Of outstanding interest is item 192, which consisted of a sheet of vellum two feet square, bearing a coloured drawing of 'Harmony' by M. Burghers, an artist who flourished at Oxford *c.* 1675. The legend surrounding the drawing consisted of twelve orders for the members of a musical club which was run by one Hall in his tavern at Oxford. The names of the forty members included Daniel Purcell, John Haslewood, Thomas Brown, John Pelling and Simon Child. This club is not mentioned by Hawkins or by Wood.[1] Ayrton's influence as a critic is attested by lot 169: 'Programme of the Worcester Festival, 1833, with a note attached addressed to Ayrton, offering a bribe.' Besides a set of the eighteenth-century Breitkopf catalogues, he had the catalogue of Burney's library in his autograph. Though not on Burney's level, Ayrton was one of the great collectors of the mid nineteenth century.

W. J. Brown is described on the title-page of the sale-catalogue simply as 'of old Bond Street'. His large collection, in 882 lots, was the first sold in the eighteen-sixties. He deserves mention because he was the earliest Victorian collector known to specialise in that old and acrimonious controversy about music in the public worship of God. Brown possessed an extensive collection of tracts on this topic, from 1660 onwards, and including some American ones of the eighteenth century. His library was also rich in unusual psalm-tune books, complemented by many scarce hymnals. But who he was, or how he came to cultivate this special taste, I have failed to discover.

In 1867 Sir George Smart died, aged ninety-one. His collection of music had been dispersed in 1860; it sheds some new light on this eminent conductor and musical administrator, who had visited Beethoven in 1825 and wrote the fascinating journal of his European travels. Smart provides yet another example of the distinguished range of Victorian interests in music. His manuscripts included 'organ fantasias'—in fact, organ parts to string consorts—by Coperario, a composer then quite out of fashion. Handel was one of Smart's great loves, and we learn from the sale-catalogue that in 1816 he prepared for a Drury Lane performance special scores of *Israel* in which he included extra items copied, by Queen Charlotte's permission, from the autograph then, apparently, at Windsor. Later, when the Royal Music

---

[1] This vellum sheet reappears as lot 173 in an anonymous sale of 2 March 1866 (S.C.P. 105(7)), when it was bought by Lonsdale for £2. 2s.

Library had been moved to Buckingham Palace, Smart made a similar recension of *Solomon* (lot 165). Morley, Meyerbeer, Haydn and Mozart all attracted Smart's collecting zeal. He seems also to have been a friend of Lord Burghersh, Earl of Westmorland, who was largely instrumental in establishing the Royal Academy of Music. Eleven lots in Smart's sale comprised operas, a Mass, glees, madrigals and four symphonies by the Earl, on which Puttick's cataloguer remarked: 'The preceding form a larger collection of the noble composer's work than is usually found in one catalogue.' Smart deserves well of posterity for keeping together a very large quantity of sale-catalogues of the numerous auctions, chiefly musical, that he attended. Many are now unique. Bound in twelve volumes, and copiously annotated, they are now preserved in the British Museum, where is also his large collection of programmes, in thirty-four volumes.

When John Hullah entrusted to Christie the sale of his music collection in 1860, he was barely forty-eight years old. (He lived to be seventy-two.) But the foundations of his great work as a popular musical educator had been well and truly laid, for between 1840 and 1860 some 25,000 persons had passed through his classes at Exeter Hall. His large library bears a vivid testimony to his work as a teacher and conductor of vocal music. Besides a mass of theory and treatises, he owned a large quantity of choral and orchestral parts. One item is described in the catalogue as 'Weber's Oberon, Second Act, choruses, 583 voices only'—a daunting thought, in terms of shelf space. The collection in general reflects such a wide range of musical sympathies that it must command respect. The second part, sold just after Hullah's death in 1884, revealed such great rarities as *Musica libris quatuor demonstrata* (Paris, 1551), Wollick's *Opus aureum musices* (1501) and Reuchlin's *Scenica progymnasmata* (1498).

Among association items cherished by Victorian collectors, it is only natural to find frequently the name of Mendelssohn, who often signed choice items in his considerable collection, and when in England regularly gave presents from it to his friends. Among them was C. E. Horsley, to whom he gave some editions of J. S. Bach. Horsley's music was, according to the title-page of the sale-catalogue of 1862, 'removed from the rooms of the Musical Society of London, comprising the collections made by W. Horsley and J. W. Callcott'. (Most of the latter's music had been sold in 1819.) It was not a very exciting library, but showed a discriminating taste for Italian cantatas of the early eighteenth century and for Italian theory of the age of Galilei and Eximeno.

The long series of sales held in the mid nineteenth century is broken by one notable gift, that which Jasper Joly made to the National Library of Ireland in 1863. Forming part of a much larger general collection, it amounted to just over 6000 items, principally of the eighteenth century, and including many single-sheet songs. Its particular strength lies in Irish and Scottish song-books, and in country dances. English and Welsh music, and ballad operas are also represented. The donor did not die until 1892.

In Edward Taylor (1784–1863) we meet one of the most influential of the great Victorian collectors. He was a bass singer from Norwich, and in 1826, after failing in his profession of civil engineer, studied music seriously and became Gresham Professor of Music in London in 1837. His lectures attracted large audiences, for he introduced into them an unusually extensive selection of music, most of which he edited from his own library. (Much of his lecture-material is now in the Royal College of Music.) Through his active work in a number of learned and semi-popular societies, his editions reached a public far wider than that of his lectures. His collection, which was sold in nearly 1000 lots in 1863, included much church music (in the history of which he specialised), numerous rare madrigals and motets, French, Italian and English. The Italians included Gesualdo, whose harmonies must have sounded very strained to Victorian ears. Taylor's copy of Wilbye's *First Set of English Madrigales* came from the Grenville Library. Another of his rarities (lot 224) seems now quite to have vanished: it was described thus: 'Forest Harmony, or the Musick of the English and French Horns, as it is now performed in the Field, Park, Forest, or chase. A large broadside, with engravings of the various animals of the chase, and musical notation of the "hunting notes".'

A much smaller sale of this same year, 1863, contained a library stated to be that of 'R. Randall, pupil of Handel'. This was perhaps Richard Randall, a tenor of Handel's later years and composer of a few songs, who had died in 1828. Randall's collection was mixed with that of one J. H. R. Chichester, otherwise unknown. Two items deserve mention—first, a copy of Archadelt's *Primo libro de' madrigali* (Rome, 1640), stated to be 'unknown to Fétis', bought, by Fétis himself, for £2. 5s.; and, second, a copy of Aristoxenus's *Harmonicorum elementorum libri III* (1562) which had belonged to the ever-venerated Pepusch.

We meet another Handelian link in the collection of one Edward Bates (sold in 1867) for he was the son of Joah Bates who was one of the founders of the Handel Commemoration of 1784. Edward Bates's taste ran to such extraordinarily diverse items as Dowland's *Micrologus* (1606), Caroso's *Il Ballarino* (1581), Praetorius's Masses and *Cantiones sacrae*, and Marcello's *Psalms*. If he does not seem to have had much concentration of purpose in his collecting, he had an eye for provenance, Hayes and Bartleman being among the names of previous owners.

The most notable Scottish collector for the first part of the mid nineteenth century was Andrew John Wighton (1804–66), a prosperous grocer of Dundee who bequeathed his music to the Town Council.[1] Wighton travelled widely in Europe to collect his music, which amounts in all to some 700 titles. He paid special attention to works of Scottish origin or association, and made copies of early manuscripts and of a number of rare printed works which are now lost.

In April 1870 a new power in music-collecting makes a brief appearance—Julian Marshall, part of whose great general library was sold anonymously by Sotheby. As it included only eight items of music, mostly early English part-books, we can better study Marshall's genius as a collector with the later sales of 1884 and 1904. In 1872 there appeared in quick succession three portions of the exceedingly rich collection of Joseph Warren (b. 1804),

[1] See H. M. Willsher, 'The Wighton Collection of National Music', in *The Review of the Activities of the Dundee Public Libraries, etc.* no. 2 (July 1948), pp. 12, 13. The collection did not become the property of the Council until 1884.

the residue being sold after his death in 1881. His most interesting autograph catalogue, which runs to 250 pages, was begun in 1849 and kept up-to-date. (It is now in the possession of Cecil Hopkinson.) The fly-leaf bears some verses by Warren, dated 3 July 1849 and beginning thus:

> My books, dear books, to thee adieu,
> I fondly hope that I may view
> Thee safely placed where no rude hands
> Can touch thee, nor in other lands
> Transplanted be—'t would break my heart
> Thee not to see or from thee part...

and so on.

These are odd sentiments from one who went on collecting for at least twenty years after 1849. We have, however, evidence from a sale-catalogue that Warren disposed of some duplicates as early as 1841. In his day, Warren was known as an editor of old music, and as a lexicographer. His collecting zeal went far beyond these needs. His autographs included Purcell, Jeremiah Clarke, Viotti, Dibdin, Mozart, Beethoven, Haydn ('Teseo mio ben'), Alessandro Scarlatti, two letters of Pepusch and over 100 songs by Hook. Among his other manuscripts were much virginal and organ music, and early operas. He had a huge quantity of theory, and paid special attention to early German, French and Dutch psalmody. His collection of sale-catalogues alone covers several pages in his tiny handwriting. Practically every period of every country is well represented in the printed music. Yet for all his hard-headed acquisitive genius, Warren was, as his verses suggest, a sentimental collector. In the preface to his catalogue he wrote:

Assuming that this is read by those deeply interested in not only musical matters in general, but versed in the knowledge of musical antiquities, I beg to point out the deep interest I have felt in this collection; for the perusal of works of a by-gone age, works that have emanated from the minds of men, who have gone before us, who have felt all that we have felt, these remains of their former greatness are but a melancholy memento of what they once were—I say I have felt a deeper interest in collecting these their works than any one can possibly imagine, and I believe few now living can appreciate this feeling.

It is as a glee composer that R. J. S. Stevens is now remembered; but we should not forget that he was also Gresham Professor from 1801 onwards. Thus it is not so surprising that his collection—sold nearly forty years after his death in 1837—included an early manuscript of Scarlatti's opera *La Rosaura*, a good deal of seventeenth-century Italian music, and a copy of the 1683 edition of Purcell's *Sonnatas of III Parts*. This passed to the Royal Academy of Music, together with his large collection of catches and glees, the manuscript index to which (partly in Stevens's own hand) was found at Cambridge in 1959 and has been acquired by the Academy.

In the mid nineteenth century, we met three aristocratic collectors of music, the Duke of Cambridge, the Duke of Sussex and the Earl of Falmouth. This distinguished tradition continues with the sixth Earl of Aylesford, whose music was auctioned in 1873, together with his notable instruments which made up one-tenth of the 430 lots. It was an assemblage well worthy of a descendant of Charles Jennens. Besides some choice early Italian theory, the Earl possessed sixteenth-century Italian organ music and the slightly later English volume from the Gauntlett Collection. Autographs of Pachelbel and of Haydn (a march in E flat), Pepusch's copy of Soriano's *Canoni* (1610), the Frankfurt Book Fair catalogues 1564–72 (probably those from Warren's library) and many Walsh scores of eighteenth-century instrumental music, were characteristic of a broadly based and discriminating taste.

The library of John Lodge Ellerton, an old Rugbeian who studied composition in Italy and later resided a good deal in Germany, was a curiously mixed bag. The occasion of its sale in 1873 was notable for the most frequent appearance hitherto of the name of W. H. Cummings among the buyers: Ellerton owned such diverse things as the autograph of an unknown Mass by Sarti, an Icelandic psalm-book of 1772, and a first edition of Beethoven's 'Battle Symphony' with corrections by Smart and papers relating to its performance by the latter at Windsor Castle. A collection of no fewer than eighty-four music sale-catalogues (some now unknown) argues a systematic interest in collecting.

Another name that appears in the sales of this crowded year 1873 is that of James Shoubridge (Vicar Choral of St Paul's and conductor of the Cecilian Society, which expired in 1858), another omnivorous collector, especially of manuscripts. He had the autograph of a 'Miserere' by Francesco Scarlatti (1714), works of Legrenzi, Carissimi and a lot of church music by G. Fenoglio. Perhaps his greatest treasure was the part of the autograph of Benjamin Cooke's diary written while he was under Pepusch's tuition from July 1746 to April 1747, and still barely fourteen years old. At an earlier anonymous sale[1] the description of this manuscript included the cataloguer's remark 'every day begins with a scriptural quotation', and gives as an example: 'Thine eye shall behold strange women, and thine heart shall write perverse things. Sunday Aug. 10. 1746. I was at the (Surrey) Chapel in the morning, but in the afternoon went to Vauxhall with the Doctor, Mrs. Pepusch being dead.' This autograph was owned by Warren, and is mentioned in his manuscript catalogue, but as it is listed in none of the four sales, Shoubridge may have acquired it privately before they took place.

Although Thomas Oliphant's collection was made up, after his death in 1873, into 594 lots, he was not, I think, a great collector. He was unsurpassed as a snapper-up of unconsidered madrigalian trifles, and amassed an astonishing number of odd parts, which fetched 3s. or 5s. each. Some of them, such as his set of Whythorne and of *Musica Transalpina* (complete, in this case) were very important, as were also the parts of various works by Claude Lejeune, which comprised nine lots. Among Oliphant's curiosities was the Sadeler print of Verdonck's *Magnificat*, about which he conjectured, rather unhappily, 'This is probably the frontispiece to a collection of sacred music'. But, as a whole, his library mirrored his career and his devoted service of nearly forty years to the Madrigal Society.

Besides the collection of R. J. S. Stevens, the later eighteen-seventies bring to notice four others which for no discoverable reason, were sold long after the death of their owners. James Hook had died at Boulogne in 1827, and it is unfortunate that nearly fifty years later Puttick mixed his

[1] 20 July 1873, lot 104 (S.C.P. 157 (7)).

music up indistinguishably with other properties. (A sale of 1842 was devoted wholly to part of Hook's collection.) But, in due time, some of it was to reappear in the collection of A. H. Mann. Crotch was more fortunate, for when most of his library came into the sale-room in 1873 (twenty-six years after his decease) and a small, rather dull residue in 1877, its identity was not lost. The chief interest of the 275 lots of the 1873 sale lies in their relation to Crotch's considerable erudition as shown in his three-volume anthology, *Specimens of various Styles of Music referred to in a course of Lectures read at Oxford and London* (Birchall, *c.* 1808–15), which reveals an immense range of musical sympathies. Another publication of Crotch's which has some bearing on his zeal as a collector is his *Substance of several Courses of Lectures*, printed in 1831. It will be remembered that he was elected Professor of Music at Oxford in 1797, having previously served at Cambridge as assistant organist at Trinity, King's and Great St Mary's. Crotch owned manuscripts of fancies from the collections of Warren-Horne and Burney, and a batch of theoretical papers in the autograph of Pepusch. Among his considerable selection of early theory we find a copy of Cerone's *Il Melopeo*. These, and some rare psalm-books, fetched fair prices at the sale: but fifty-one copies of his oratorio *The Revival of the Hope of Israel* made only 2s. the lot.

The third of these delayed sales was that of the collection of A. F. C. Kollmann, which took place in 1877, forty-eight years after his death. It was not a very distinguished library, but interesting for the various editions and copies of J. S. Bach which he had amassed, mostly during his forty-five years residence in London. Some of the books clearly reflect his special interest in the theory of music. His Mozart included various André editions, presented to him by that publisher, with an autograph dedication. Some of these copies ultimately reached the Hirsch Library, and two more are in my own possession. The last section of this 1877 sale seems to have included some property not Kollmann's: one curious item deserves mention —'Handel's Ruffle, exquisitely embroidered in fine Cambric. In a glass case. The only portion of Handel's clothing extant.' This ruffle reappeared in the

Cummings sale in 1917 (lot 825) when it was bought for £10. 10s. by Phillips.

I must mention briefly the small music collection of Thomas Moore which comprised but nine lots of his library sold in 1874, twenty-seven years after his decease. The most interesting item shows that he had some interest in Mozart, for he possessed all the major operas and the Requiem in a uniform Paris edition, probably that issued by Schlesinger in about 1822.

The harvest of the eighteen-seventies includes the name of William Euing, an underwriter and insurance broker who bequeathed his famous collection to Anderson's College in Glasgow, where it is now one of the great glories of the University Library. In 1876, two years after Euing's death, appeared the notorious anonymous catalogue, which nevertheless gives a fair idea of his wonderful judgement and enterprise in collecting. The scope and quality of the library are well enough known to make any description superfluous, but it must be emphasised that well over two thousand items consist of theoretical works, many of very great rarity. In this respect it is one of the richest individual collections in Britain.

As a collector Sterndale Bennett seems to have been a curious mixture. While he seems to have had little interest in musical theory and history, he amassed much that had a strong association value. He kept a specially bound set of the Beethoven complete edition presented to him in 1865 by the directors of the Gewandhaus at Leipzig. As might be expected, he had a lot of Mendelssohn, including the autograph of the 'Hebrides' overture (here described as the 'Isles of Fingal'), purchased for £52—a high price—by that enterprising collector Taphouse, who also bought thirteen autograph letters of Mendelssohn to the publisher Coventry, an album containing autographs of Beethoven, Goethe and Mozart, and Bennett's autograph annotated catalogue of his own collection. That he also had an interest in older music is indicated by a special manuscript copy of the Fitzwilliam music (presumably Novello's edition), some early Purcell editions and some Playford. The first sale, of 1875, also contained a good deal of J. S. Bach, an interest probably due to friendship with Mendelssohn. The second, and much less interesting, part of Bennett's collection was sold in 1878.

In scholarly interest, one of the most outstanding of the Victorian collections was that of Edward Francis Rimbault, who died in 1876. His books and music were sold in two portions, by Sotheby, in 1877. (A note in his hand of a 'gift to Warren' is reproduced in Pl. VIII.) Of the 2259 lots, nearly half is music and musical literature. The preponderance of English works of the seventeenth century testified to Rimbault's special interest as editor. Whatever the quality of his editions, he had an unquestionable flair for sources—the Mulliner Book, John Sambrooke's manuscript anthology of 'Motets and Anthems', *Parthenia Inviolata*, and so on. The last-named volume was bought by Sabin, who secured other rarities which, like that *Parthenia*, were destined for American libraries. Rimbault's curiosa included a manuscript headed: 'A Demonstration of ye Feasability of making a machine that shall write extempore Voluntarys or other musick as fast as any master of musick shall be able to play them upon the organ, harpsichord, etc.'[1] He also had a copy of that now lost pamphlet published by the Academy of Ancient Music in 1732, *Letters to Signor Lotti with his answers and testimonies*.

There was of course the less desirable side to Rimbault's acquisitive nature —his abstraction of various rarities from the Christ Church Library in the early eighteen-forties. But as this, and their sale to the British Museum, has been described by W. G. Hiscock,[2] I shall not enlarge on the matter here. Rimbault seems to have been something of a by-word among his fellow collectors. For otherwise there would be little point in the satire, attributed by Taphouse to R. Lonsdale, which appeared in 1862 with the title *Catalogue of the extensive Library of Dr. Rainbeau...which Messrs. Topsy, Turvy, & Co. will put up for public competition*.[3] The humour is mostly reminiscent of the Lower Fifth, but there is a pleasant parody of the nineteenth-century mania for 'authentic' editions of Beethoven. Lot 91 comprises 'Beethoven's

---

[1] Now Drexel MS. 4322 in New York Public Library.
[2] 'Christ Church Missing Books', *Times Literary Supplement*, 11 February 1939.
[3] Copy in the Hirsch Library (B.M.), IV. 1452a.

works, complete from the author's MSS'; lots 92–100, 'Beethoven's works, the most correct', edited—or published—by Moscheles, Bennett, Potter, Hallé, Sloper, Liszt, French, Artaria; lots 101–103, 'Beethoven's works, the best editions, edited by Hummel, Czerny, Kalkbrenner'.

One of the treasures in the small collection of George Townshend Smith, organist of Hereford Cathedral, was the autograph of Haydn's cantata *Arianna in Naxos*. At Smith's sale in 1877 it seems to have passed to Christopher Lonsdale, a collector of unusual interest. Before establishing his own publishing business, he had been a partner in Birchall, Lonsdale & Mills, the firm which originated in 1783 as Birchall & Andrews. This Lonsdale had kept Beethoven's correspondence with Birchall, adding thereto his own drafts of letters to Beethoven. Other documents relating to music-publishing included Kozeluch's correspondence with Bland and Birchall, Cramer's assignments to Birchall, and some Clementi autographs. In 1862 Lonsdale received from Köchel a signed copy of his thematic catalogue of Mozart. He also owned a set of Farrenc's *Trésor des pianistes*, which was purchased by Sabin. No fewer than forty-five lots in his remarkable collection comprised printed and manuscript music of Sir Henry Bishop. Sotheby's sale-catalogue of 1878 is altogether one of exceptional interest.

Another name of the period now virtually unknown is Frederick Smee, a minor composer of sacred music, who is described in the sale-catalogue of 1879 as 'of Arundel Villas, Balham, and the Bank of England'. His fair-sized collection—396 lots—included much early Purcell, Anglebert's *Pièces de clavecin*, and the autograph of Handel's *Amadigi*, seventy-three folios, purchased by Julian Marshall for £35, but since lost. It does not appear in any of the catalogues of the four Marshall sales. This autograph was not traced by William C. Smith to a date later than 1870. (There were included with it two testimonies to its authenticity, one signed by Rimbault, and both based on comparison with other autographs at Buckingham Palace.) Smee also possessed Mozart's String Quintet in D (this, by the way, being an ownership unknown to Köchel-Einstein; the autograph is now owned by Olga Hirsch), and a copy of Travers's *Eighteen Canzonets* presented by

Pepusch to Andrew Strother. The Rome edition of John Ravenscroft's *Sonate à tre* is another choice piece indicative of Smee's feeling for rarity. Only two copies of it are now known in British libraries.

At some unknown date before his death in 1880, John Fitchett Marsh 'deposited, by way of loan' his distinguished collection of music in the Warrington Museum and Library. Though not very large—it made up into 381 lots—it is a great pity that it was ever withdrawn and sold, for it was rich in unusual pieces, principally English, of the seventeenth and early eighteenth century, such as Gamble's *Ayres and Dialogues* (1656), and Crotch's own copy of the Walsh edition of Handel's organ concertos. A few earlier works included the Venice (1549) edition of the *Compendium musices*. I have not found any other instance of a nineteenth-century collector depositing his treasures in a public library.

The name of the earlier Carl Engel is now known for his study of instruments, for his catalogues of the collection in what is now the Victoria and Albert Museum, and for his interest in ancient music and folk music. It is curious that his extensive collection of musical literature, sold in two parts —one just before, and the other shortly after, his death in 1882—reflects faithfully the latter but hardly at all the former. He possessed a lot of musical theory, and a great wealth of books on and collections of folk music, especially that of the Slavonic countries. He seems to have had some interest in string chamber music, for a small but select group of it included the Roger edition of Caix d'Hervelois's *Pièces de viole*, and Finger's *Sonatae xii*, in the Amsterdam (1688) edition.

A certain W. Laidlaw of Liverpool, whose collection was sold in 1883, specialised in vocal music, such as the autograph of Boyce's Funeral Anthem for George II, and a manuscript of a Mass by Pergolesi, both formerly owned by William Hayes. That he also had some bibliographical interest in music is suggested by a set of the eighteenth-century Breitkopf catalogues, which Schott acquired for 11s.

With Julian Marshall, whom I have mentioned briefly before, we reach one of the greatest of all British collectors. The prodigious richness of his

1 (a) *A dated note of ownership in the autograph of Thomas Hamond*

1 (b) *A dated note of ownership in the autograph of Viscount Fitzwilliam*

II (a)  *The signed bookplate of John Stanley*

II (b)  *The bookplate designed by Granville Sharp*

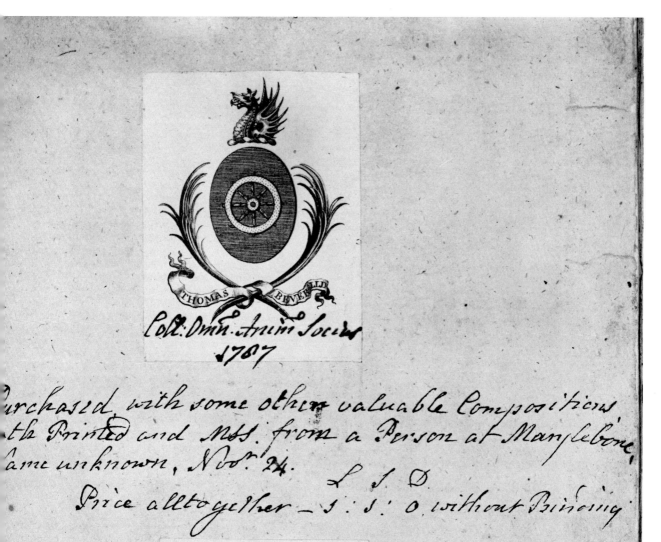

THOMAS BEVER

Coll: Omn: Anim: Socius
1787

Purchased with some other valuable Compositions
both Printed and MSS. from a Person at Marylebone
Name unknown, Nov.r 24.
                              L S D
        Price alltogether — s : s : o without Binding

III *The dated bookplate of Thomas Bever, with a note in his autograph*

After all my just Debts are paid, I give
and bequeath to George, my eldest Son
the Sum of Fifty Pound Sterling, and also
my large Gold Snuff Box, which was a Present
to me from The Queen, / send me by Mrs.
Swellenberg on the Day The Prince of Wales
was born, / and which on that Account I value
highly, and wish it to be kept in my Family.
— Item to Mary, my said Sons Wife, I bequeath
the Sum of Ten Guineas, to buy any little
Article She likes.

IV *A passage from the autograph will of Frederick Nicolay*

Here, the Recit: — O Barack —

The Duet — Where do thy Ardours raise me —

the Chorus — Forbear thy Doubts. —

the Recit: — Since Heaven has thus —

the Chorus — For ever to the Voice of Prayer

the Recit: — By that adorable Degree. —

are wanting. —

*A list of lacunae in vol. II of the autograph score of Handel's* Deborah, *written by Frederick Nicolay*

*This Volume belongs to The Queen.*
*1788.*

*Giulii's Sonatas. — Op: 4.*
*Schobert's — Three Quatuor. — Op: 7.ᵗʰ*
*Eichner's Sonatas.*
*Giordani's Quintetti.*
*A Concerto by Paradies.*
*Filtz's Sonatas. — Op: 2?*

VI *An index, in the autograph of Frederick Nicolay, to a volume of printed music owned by Queen Charlotte*

VII *A page of the* Mulliner Book, *with a note in the autograph of John Stafford Smith*

Joseph Warren, the gift of his friend
Edward F Rimbault, July 30/1840

*late*

They had quarrelled over
some rascality or other, – I think it
was the forgery in "God save the King"
in Clark's book.

J.M.

VIII *A note of presentation in the autograph of Edward Francis Rimbault,
with an explanatory note signed: J.M. (i.e. Julian Marshall)*

music library as a whole can only be grasped from a study of the catalogues of the two Sotheby sales of 1884 in conjunction with the final sale of 1904, held a year after his death.[1] Yet the curious thing is that Marshall was not wholly a specialist in music. He was born in 1836, and must have amassed considerable wealth from the family flax-spinning business that he owned in Leeds. He wrote the *Annals of Tennis* and possessed many books on the subject. Card-games and gaming in general were other objects of his book-collecting. He contributed some articles to Grove, as did also his wife Florence. But his music library went far beyond these modest needs. In the sales of 1884 it amounted to 127 lots of autograph letters in the first sale, and 1339 lots in the second. In the 1904 sale, a total of 622 lots of his general library included almost ninety lots of music—principally sets of parts, somewhat imperfect, of music by Elizabethan and Stuart composers.

Marshall's music collection was predominantly English, including many Playford rarities and many association-pieces—a copy of Purcell's *Ode to St Cecilia* (1683), with autograph corrections; Queen Anne's copy of *Divine Harmony*; Horace Walpole's copy of Mace; Muffat's *Componimenti musicali*, *c.* 1730, in a fine-paper copy specially dedicated to Charles IV; Hiller's *Die verwandelten Weiber* 'from the library of the Queen in 1788'[2] with bookplate of the Princess Sophia; Anglebert's *Pièces de clavecin* with the composer's autograph receipt for 60 livres for playing the clavecin in the *Ballet de la naissance de Vénus*; fourteen vocal scores of Rossini operas from the library of King Otho of Greece—and so on.

Marshall also had some interest in English opera, as evinced, *inter alia*, by three Covent Garden lists and cash books, for 1740, 1759 and 1760. His autograph documents included a receipt of Thomas Ford, dated 20 November 1618; letters from Pepusch to Immyns; and letters by Stephen and Anna Storace (Stephen's described his journey from London to Vienna). All these lots, and numerous others, were bought by Cummings, who was now nearing his zenith as a collector. To the best of my knowledge, Marshall

---

[1] In 1880–1 the British Museum acquired privately many important manuscripts, now Add. 31384–31823, which were therefore never catalogued for auction.

[2] Presumably Nicolay's inscription.

was the first who had rarities of music bound by Bedford, in the full calf with distinctive mottled endpapers that make his books recognisable at a glance. He often annotated his books, as is shown in Pl. VIII.

Two lesser collectors deserve brief notice, W. H. Husk and the Earl of Westmorland. Husk was, of course, the immensely industrious librarian of the Sacred Harmonic Society, and contributed to the first edition of *Grove* many excellent, if slightly waspish articles on English musicians. His personal library was a sound, working collection, with a reasonable bias towards his special interest in English musical history. The catalogue of 1887 reveals no special rarities, but he did amass many music sale-catalogues, dated from 1813 to 1868, and had them bound in eight volumes. The Earl of Westmorland's collection, sold also in 1887, was a good deal larger, and, rather like those of the Duke of Sussex and the Earl of Falmouth some thirty-five years earlier, reveals a curiously mixed taste. He leavened a good deal of Spohr and Onslow with such choice things as a manuscript score of Haydn's 'Missa S. Johannis', with corrections and additions stated to be in the composer's autograph (1786). Another unusual item was an engraver's manuscript of Beethoven's trio, op. 3, with notes in the autograph of the composer—a type of document which is now of the greatest rarity. All trace of this manuscript seems to have been lost.

It may be stretching a point to include J. H. Mapleson among collectors of music, but he was at any rate the first in England ever to have specialised in operatic material, albeit for the work of his own company. The catalogues of two sales should perhaps be considered in conjunction with his vastly entertaining *Memoirs*, but they are rather disappointing. A collection described as 'extensive' and sold in 1888 comprised only forty-three rather dull lots, and is mixed up with the theatrical wardrobe of Her Majesty's Theatre, catalogued according to operas. The costumes for *Faust* included such lots as '1 Valentine, 1 Wagner, and 1 strip dress with hats and belts'. A second sale ran to thirty-two lots of operatic material—each comprising a full score, vocal scores, and parts for band and chorus. Nearly all were bought by another member of the family for ludicrous prices; the *Flying*

*Dutchman* material, for instance, made but £2. 6s. The whole Mapleson collection was much larger than this, but a good deal seems to have rotted away.[1] In 1946 there were piles of it to be seen stacked in a very damp shed, at the end of a garden in Camden Town.

After so much ebb and flow during the course of the nineteenth century, it is pleasant to encounter solid ground once more in the shape of another noble bequest—the collection of Sir Frederick Ouseley, which passed, after his death in 1889, to his own foundation, St Michael's College, Tenbury. Part of this magnificent assemblage of music and musical literature has been described in print by its collector[2] and the whole in more detail by Canon E. H. Fellowes.[3] The numerous important manuscripts are also known from Fellowes's catalogue of 1934. An attempt to summarise here the treasures of the collection is as unnecessary as it would be absurd. Suffice it to say that these 3000 volumes—1000 or so of theory and history, the rest of music —probably represent the genius of the Victorian collector at its highest point, in range, variety and quality. It is fascinating to study the sale-catalogues from the eighteen-fifties onwards, and to see Ouseley's name as the purchaser of one rare item after another. Besides being well served by dealers, as Fellowes points out, he undoubtedly bid himself at numerous auctions. Ouseley's vision as to what was important—in both manuscript and print—for the study of musicology was amazing, but entirely worthy of one who introduced such important reforms in the teaching of music while Professor at Oxford from 1855 onwards. Ouseley's particular interest in Spanish music is related to his privately issued anthology *Motets by Spanish composers arranged to illustrate lectures on the Church Music of Spain* (4 books, Oxford, *c.* 1880). At his papers read to the Musical Association, Ouseley exhibited numerous specimens from his collection, and during one of the

---

[1] An earlier disposal of some of the Mapleson property took place on 21 February 1881, when a mixed sale (S.C.P. 201 (5)) included (lots 215–384) operatic performing material belonging to 'the late Mrs Mapleson senior'.

[2] In *Proceedings of the Musical Association*, 'On the early Italian and Spanish Treatises on Counterpoint and Harmony', session 5, 3 March 1879, and 'On some Italian and Spanish Treatises on Music of the Seventeenth Century', session 8, 6 February 1882.

[3] See *History of St Michael's College, Tenbury*, edited by M. F. Alderson and H. C. Colles (London, 1943), pp. 78–101.

discussions he assured Sir John Stainer that he had read all his rare works of musical theory right through. How many others could say the same?

An important specialist collector of this time was John Dobson, of Richmond and formerly of Manchester, whose library of psalms and hymns was sold in 1889 in 492 lots. He had many rare French and German books and a copy of Day's *Psalms in Foure Parts* (1563) purchased by 'Novello' for £36.

Andrew George Kurtz was secretary of the Liverpool Philharmonic Society, and when his collection of autographs was dispersed by Sotheby in 1895, nearly half of it comprised music, both letters and compositions. Kurtz bequeathed a large collection of letters, including many by musicians, to the British Museum (now Add. 33964–5). He also specialised in musical portraits and caricatures. He had undoubtedly a flair for the unusual and important—such as Mozart's Rondo in A minor (£28) and variations on 'La bergère Celimène' (£32. 12s.). But the cataloguing is sometimes vague —for example, lot 64: 'Beethoven, Original autograph music'—and not all the works can be identified.

The total number of music collectors whom I have mentioned by name or passed in review since the time of William Heather is 127. Of these, thirty-two belonged to the seventeenth and eighteenth centuries; the remainder, to a total of ninety-five (including those who gave or bequeathed their collections intact), are of the nineteenth century. This period I have treated very selectively as regards collectors whose music was auctioned

|  | Named sales | Anonymous sales |
|---|---|---|
| 1801–1830 | 44 | 12 |
| 1831–1840 | 6 | — |
| 1841–1850 | 30 | 7 |
| 1851–1860 | 29 | 2 |
| 1861–1870 | 16 | 11 |
| 1871–1880 | 37 | 14 |
| 1881–1890 | 33 | 5 |
| 1891–1900 | 1 | — |
|  | 196 | 51 |

either under their own name or anonymously. The complete figures for such sales, given at the foot of p. 68, are very striking. (I exclude all sales of plates, copyrights and the like.)

Thus, in the seventy years from 1830 to 1900, there were 191 sales of the property of music collectors, named and unnamed, and of these 89 were concentrated in the years from 1871 to 1890. Clearly, the Victorians collected music on a scale which was never known before and can never be repeated again in this country. Even in the small collections which I have had to leave unmentioned, there is usually at least a handful of old, unusual items. The truth is that, even without the Third Programme, high-fidelity recording and extra-mural lectures, the Victorian lover of music had often developed a much wider sense of its historical values than has hitherto been generally allowed. It is only natural for this to be reflected in the collecting of music, which, even before the end of the era, begins to presage the very different character that it has assumed in the last sixty years.

## LECTURE IV

# TRENDS OF THE TWENTIETH CENTURY: SOME GHOSTS AND PRICES

A sufficient number of the great Victorian collectors lived on into the first two decades of the new era to invest it with a certain Elgarian splendour, but they were the last of their kind. The distant music that accompanies the closing scenes of this pageant is thus tinged with regret for the passing of the tradition so handsomely maintained by Ayrton and Ouseley, by Rimbault and Warren.

The pace of the acquisition and dispersal of music during the second and third quarters of the nineteenth century was too hot to last. Even the reduced number of those collecting after 1900 were faced with increased competition in the sale-room from institutional libraries belatedly building up their holdings and from European and American collectors. There simply were not enough important manuscripts and rare early editions to go round: prices rose. The scholar could no longer afford the outlay made by, say, Vincent Novello, on a large library for his personal research. Therefore the whole scope of twentieth-century music-collecting has gradually shrunk and changed direction. But, as always, change brings compensation: in this case, a twofold benefit—a rapid rise in specialised collecting (both subject and composer), and a notable increase, as welcome as it is unaccountable, in the number of gifts and bequests.

It would be difficult, even were it still desirable, for me to maintain the same uniform chronological order as hitherto. I propose now to divide collectors into two main groups—first, those whose music was sold by auction or private treaty, keeping general collectors separate from the specialists and extending both categories to cover those still active today; second, those whose music was transmitted intact, or largely so, by gift, sale or bequest. Then, after an excursion on the theme—sentimental, perhaps, but still fascinating—of ghosts, I shall conclude with an attempted survey of prices.

The famous Taphouse Collection was sold by Sotheby[1] in July 1905, in 876 lots. As befitted the collector's business in Oxford, the music was mostly printed, save for a few things like the (now lost) manuscript of a Purcell violin sonata later owned by Cummings and Miss E. A. Willmott, and the autographs of Bishop's lectures. Taphouse had something of most periods, especially a good deal of Purcell, of psalmody and early theory. It is worth mentioning that 123 of the lots were acquired by Leeds Public Libraries.[2] Many of Taphouse's treasures came from Warren, Crotch, Rimbault, Bennett, and Marshall.

In the preface to the typescript catalogue[3] of his library James E. Matthew stated that 'the object which he has kept steadily in view, has been to make a collection which should be of help in all departments of musical research. ...No other library that has hitherto been collected, with the exception of that formed by the late M. J. Fétis...will be found to compare with it in this particular.' Amounting to nearly 6000 volumes, rich especially in pamphlets and ephemera, this notable collection was bought by Liepmannssohn in 1906 and dispersed. Matthew left a lively account of some of his treasures in his book entitled *The Literature of Music*.[4]

W. H. Cummings, who died in 1915 at the age of 84, after a long career as a leading tenor, teacher and administrator, was the last of the far-ranging Victorians. His collection was sold on six days in May 1917 in 1744 lots, which included a little general history and literature. There was hardly any composer, theorist or musical biographer of the first or second rank not represented, in both print and manuscript. There were some 150 lots of

---

[1] This firm captured the auctioning of music from Puttick & Simpson in the twentieth century. Henceforward I shall not mention the firm of auctioneers unless it was other than them.

[2] See also: 'The Musical Library of Mr T. W. Taphouse M.A.' by 'Dotted Crotchet', in *Musical Times*, October 1904, pp. 629–36.

[3] *c.* 1905. Copy in B.M. Hirsch 463.

[4] London, 1896: one of 'The Book-Lover's Library'. Matthew also described his collection in a paper printed in the *Proceedings of the Musical Association*: 'Some Notes on Musical Libraries, and on that of the writer in particular', session 29 (1902/3), pp. 139–68.

autograph letters and manuscripts; sixty lots of Handel editions and manuscripts, and thirty-five of psalms. This monumental assemblage should be considered in the light of the highly interesting paper which he read to the Musical Association in 1877, 'On the Formation of a national musical Library'. Many of his treasures can no longer be traced: where are lot 108 'Ben. Cooke. Catalogue of Music Books in the little Wainscot Case. 5¼ pp.', or lot 594 'The Diverting Post 1705/6: songs in verse only'? A residue of some 400 choice pieces were purchased ultimately by Marquis Tokugawa and went to Nanki Library in Tokyo; after the Second World War they passed into the ownership of Kyubei Okhi.

The famous music of the eighth Earl of Aylesford formed lots 201 to 326*c* of the sale of his library held in May 1918. It was a survival from the eighteenth century to which there is only one true parallel in our own times. Prices, towards the end of the war, were even lower than those of the Cummings sale. The collection was of course especially rich in J. C. Smith and other manuscript copies of Handel, and in music of his Italian contemporaries. Many valuable Handel copies were acquired by Newman (later Sir Newman) Flower, and others were bought by Squire for addition to the King's Music Library (as the Royal Music was then called).

A. H. Littleton, for many years chairman of Messrs Novello and Company, specialised in early German and Italian theory, with a leavening of psalters from the sixteenth century and some service-books from the fifteenth. At the sale in May 1918 the 200 lots fetched relatively much higher prices than those from the Aylesford Collection. For instance, Senfl's *Liber selectarum cantionum* (1520) went for £50: Watson's *Madrigals* (1590) for £46, and the Byrd and Tallis *Cantiones* (1575) for £36. Some of the choicest items of musical theory were acquired for the library of London University.

The general library of Sir Frederick Bridge, sold at Hodgson's in July 1924, included some eighty lots of music, some good early Purcell editions, Salter's *Genteel Companion* (1683) which fetched £30, and the copy of the second part of *Youth's Delight on the Flagelet* which, then misidentified as

Greeting's *Pleasant Companion* and without mention of Pepys's ownership, made only £3. 5s.[1] By far the most interesting lot was 530, the autograph of the famous exercises which Attwood wrote under Mozart's supervision. It was sold for £110.

Another Hodgson sale, in June 1925, was devoted to the little-known collection of the singer and writer W. A. Barrett (1836–91), which had received some additions from his son F. E. H. J. Barrett, the music editor of the *Morning Post*. The music comprised lots 321–631 and included a quantity of eighteenth-century vocal works, especially glees, the tenor parts of some madrigals believed to be in the hand of Weelkes (probably the so-called 'Weelkes Commonplace Book', now in the Folger Library, Washington, D.C.), and some scarce musical literature such as H. Thorowgood's *Description of the Aeolian Harp* (n.d.) and Joshua Steele's *Account of a musical Instrument from the South Seas* (1775).

After Frank Kidson's death in 1926, his collection of some 4000 items, many bearing his bibliographical annotations, was kept together. Most of it, including his vast index of airs in fifty-seven volumes, ultimately passed to the Mitchell Library in Glasgow: a small residue, including some manuscript catalogues and notebooks, is in the Central Library of his native city, Leeds. His work as a collector centred on his publication of old English songs and dances, and on his great book on British music publishers.[2]

In December 1934 Hodgson sold the general library of Sir John Stainer who had died in 1901. Lots 636–768 comprised his music, and an extraordinary mixture it was. Early theory and church music, Diruta's *Il Transilvano* (£4. 5s.) and the *Bird Fancier's Delight* of 1730, rub shoulders with some English song-books, Caroso's *Il Ballarino*, and a slightly imperfect copy of the 1651 edition of *The Dancing Master*. The song-books were the residue of Stainer's famous collection (acquired by Walter N. H. Harding in 1932) of which he had issued a privately printed catalogue in 1891. He also amassed many now rare nineteenth-century hymn-books:

[1] It is now in the British Museum.
[2] See H. G. Farmer, 'The Kidson Collection', in *The Consort*, July 1950, pp. 12–17.

most of these were not auctioned but seem to have passed to Church House, Westminster, and are now in the British Museum.

The two segments of the Edward Speyer Collection which were auctioned in June and July 1940 were but the visible part of the iceberg. They included fifty-one lots of first and early editions of Beethoven, and some good autograph letters, but the vast bulk of this superlative collection had been purchased by Heinrich Eisemann in 1935, the year after Speyer died aged ninety-five. He acquired most of his treasures after he became a British subject in 1869. As listed by Otto Haas for valuation they amounted to nearly 500 items of autographs, music, autograph letters, manuscript copies corrected by composers, documents and association items. While the German classics predominated, practically every other composer and every singer or performer of distinction, from Bach to Verdi, was represented.[1]

Miss E. A. Willmott was the last of the few women who have collected music, which she did with taste and discrimination. Lots 383–575 at the sale of her library in April 1935 included good autographs of music or documents by Lully, J. S. Bach, Gluck, Mozart, Schubert, Mendelssohn, Liszt and others. She also had some fine copies of Elizabethan and Stuart part-books, including a copy of the second edition of Morley's *Canzonets* (1606), formerly owned by Joseph Haslewood and Taphouse, which went for £39. Among the few books on music was the now very rare anonymous *Essay upon the Use of Organs in Christian Assemblies* (1713).[2]

The flame of the great Victorian collectors flickered once more to life in G. E. P. Arkwright (1864–1944). His music was sold in two portions, the chief in February 1939[3] and the residue in December 1944. The chief portion was in 301 lots, mostly single items, well worthy of the editor of *The Musical Antiquary* and the *Old English Edition*. The music was largely printed and predominantly English, but with a fine representation of early Italian theory and church music, some German seventeenth-century part-books,

---

[1] Many of the choicest items were exhibited at the *Sunday Times Book Exhibition* of 1934, of which a catalogue was published.

[2] Reprinted at Glasgow in 1865.

[3] Not 1929, as in *Grove*, 'Collections, private'.

many first editions of Handel, and such choice things as Pepusch's copy of Bevin's *Introduction* of 1631, and Philips's *Libro primo de madrigali* (Phalèse, 1596) of which four parts out of five made but £4. 10s.—perhaps a hint of impending wartime prices.

Although, unlike Edward Speyer, Paul Hirsch did not settle in England until comparatively late in life, his place among the great British collectors is secured not merely by the fact of his own naturalisation, but even more by the numerous important additions he made to his library from 1936 onwards and by the endless generosity with which he made it available to students. The range and quality of the Hirsch Music Library are fully known from his own catalogues and from the supplementary publications of the British Museum. It need only be recorded here that when it was acquired by the Museum in 1946, Cambridge's loss was the nation's gain.

When Gerald M. Cooper died in 1947, he bequeathed his large collection to E. J. Dent; the latter presented it mostly to the Central Music Library and gave smaller portions to the Fitzwilliam Museum and the Pendlebury Library. Cooper's interests centred on old English and Italian music, especially of the period of Purcell, from whose works he edited for the Purcell Society a *Popular Edition of Selected Music*. His collection also bears on his *Tudor Edition of Old Music* (1924), which included music by Caccini and the English lutenists.

The sale of Arthur F. Hill's collection took place in June 1947, seven years after his decease. The 330 lots, many in Rivière bindings, fetched £10,187, a high total but one indicative of the quality of the whole and of the rise in prices. While naturally paying special attention to violin music, both solo and for chamber groups, of the seventeenth and eighteenth centuries, Hill had specialised in English editions—those of Playford particularly—in portraits of musicians, and in visiting cards, of which 250 comprised lot 235. Lots 241–323 were made up of autograph music, letters and documents. The collection as a whole shows an unusual degree of judgement and concentration of purpose.

The same cannot altogether be said of E. H. W. Meyerstein, whose music formed lots 279–378 in the sale of 15–17 December 1952. Some good Beethoven first and early editions were almost the only focal point in an extraordinarily heterogeneous collection of printed music, much of it in indifferent condition. His autographs, on the other hand, were distinguished, and he generously bequeathed the most choice to the Department of Manuscripts in the British Museum,[1] in which he served as an Assistant Keeper from 1913 to 1918. This bequest, including autographs of works by Haydn, Mozart, Beethoven, Schubert, Hummel, Mendelssohn and Chopin, fairly reflected his lifelong personal enthusiasm.

No account of the general collectors of this period would be complete without some mention of H. J. Laufer, who died in 1956. His sympathies were very wide: he ranged from the early musical productions of the presses of his native Bohemia up to the rarities of the classical and romantic periods from Handel to Berlioz, with especial emphasis on C. P. E. Bach, J. S. Bach, Mozart and Liszt, to a total of over 1000. His flair for the unusual led him to acquire the autograph of an unpublished Scarlatti oratorio, *Il Primo omicidio*, and two leaves written in Leopold Mozart's hand, containing the earliest of all Mozart's works, of which the very existence had remained unknown for nearly two centuries. Regrettably, his premature death caused his treasures to be scattered.[2]

During the twentieth century a number of eminent British critics amassed collections of music: Deutsch mentions Fuller-Maitland, Colles, Fox Strangways, and the younger Edwin Evans (whose music was ultimately acquired by the Central Music Library). To them may be added Bonavia and Newman. But, with two partial exceptions, it is difficult to rate them as true collectors. Fuller-Maitland's sale revealed only twenty-eight lots, mainly of musical literature, but he did also collect some good English manuscripts, chiefly of church music from the late seventeenth century to the mid eighteenth. These he bequeathed to Lancaster County Library, whence they have been transferred on indefinite loan to Liverpool Uni-

---

[1] See B. Schofield and C. E. Wright, 'The Meyerstein Bequest' in *The British Museum Quarterly*, vol. XVIII, no. 4 (December 1953).

[2] A good many have appeared in the catalogues of Hermann Baron.

versity Library. Newman acquired a considerable quantity of special literature bearing directly or indirectly on Wagner and his period. But in general
English critics do not seem to have frequented the sale-room or to have
studied catalogues. The position of a critic may often bring for review a
continual flow of music and musical literature. Without disrespect to this
profession, I feel that such a process of passive acquisition as this, blameless
indeed in itself, rather resembles that of the jub-jub

> who stands at the door
> And collects, though he does not subscribe.

The specialist collectors of this century have few counterparts in earlier
times. Many of them possessed a good deal of English church music, but
none devoted himself wholly to it as did John S. Bumpus, who, shortly
before he died in 1913, expressed some anxiety lest his collection should be
dispersed. But he gave no clear instructions about its destination, and it
seems ultimately to have been scattered, together with his library of literature on the subject. A ten-page list in his hand, headed 'Sacred Music with
English Words'[1] certainly does not represent the whole. The collection was,
of course, formed in connection with the book *A History of English Cathedral
Music*, which he wrote in collaboration with his twin brother.

At Great Bookham, in Surrey, there died in 1913 Adolph Schloesser, a
minor composer and a professor at the Royal Academy who settled in London in 1854 and seems to be known as a specialist collector only from
Squire's mention of him in the second edition of *Grove* (s.v. Libraries). He
was the son of Louis Schloesser, *Hofkapellmeister* of Darmstadt and a pupil
of Salieri, and possibly inherited from him most of his collection. It
included autographs of almost all the nineteenth-century masters. Squire
annotated the entry in *Grove* with 'sold?': but I have failed to trace a sale.

The tale of the specialists whose music was definitely sold begins with
S. R. Christie-Miller. I have been unable to ascertain whether he had the
interest in music required for the inclusion in these lectures of one who was

---

[1] B.M. Add. MS. 50202, which also comprises a typed letter expressing his anxiety, as above. Grove
(2nd ed. 1906) lists a number of the choicer items.

also a general collector on a large scale. Since his music was of such high quality and was all catalogued separately for a single sale, in December 1919, he must clearly be included although perhaps as the exception that proves my rule. The 166 lots comprised most of the original and early editions of all the English masters of madrigal and song active during the late Eliza-bethan and early Stuart period. Besides these, John Forbes of Aberdeen was represented by four editions of his *Cantus* and one of his *Psalm Tunes*. The prices were sensational, presumably because of the presence of the American dealer George D. Smith among the buyers.

Alfred Moffat, who died in 1950, was well known as an editor of for-gotten chamber music of the eighteenth century. His notable collection was acquired by Otto Haas in 1944 and offered for sale in his catalogue no. 20. It amounted to over 700 items, many of very great scarcity, mostly English, but including some French pieces, and some song-books including a *Bellerophon* of 1633. Much of the collection was acquired by the Library of Congress: the British Museum made a modest purchase.

W. Westley Manning was undeniably a general collector of manuscripts but as, at the sale of his property in October 1955, 148 of the 502 lots com-prised music, he can hardly be omitted. Music was among the treasures he acquired in boyhood, and for all the seventy years of his activity as a col-lector, it kept a high place in his interest. He succeeded in finding an auto-graph composition or document written by most of the great masters from Byrd to Richard Strauss. (The Byrd letter is now B.M. Egerton MS. 3722.)

I feel some hesitancy in including E. J. Dent among the ranks of collectors, for I fancy he might have described them, with few exceptions, in much the same terms as Housman used of bibliophiles—'an idiotic class'. Neverthe-less, Dent did amass much music and musical literature of great historical interest (sold in January 1958) with especial emphasis on his lifelong love— opera. One of his choicest things was Florence Nightingale's collection of thirty-seven libretti of operas which she heard in London or in Italy between 1835 and 1843 and which she annotated with comments on costume and action.

From about 1920 onwards C. B. Oldman began to collect on two fronts—Mozart and musical bibliography. His extensive collection of the literature on Mozart's life and works and of contemporary and early editions of his music bore fruit in many articles and reviews; the by-product, as it were, came later in the form of pioneer studies in musical bibliography, mostly written in collaboration with others and bearing especially on the period from about 1780 to 1850. Part of Oldman's collection was auctioned in May 1959; some early Mozart editions and a quantity of Mozart literature were disposed of to Hermann Baron: the latter, to a total of some 300 items, appeared in his catalogue no. 53 of 1961. Oldman presented to the British Museum a goodly residue of printed music, by Mozart, Haydn, Beethoven and their English contemporaries.

In the same period Harold Reeves (d. 1961) was active as a collector specialising in autograph letters and historical documents of musical interest. When dispersed by auction in December 1960 they comprised seventy-three lots, ranging from C. P. E. Bach to Richard Strauss. One lot comprised over 1000 letters, and there were besides eight of Mendelssohn, five of Liszt and twenty-six of Saint-Saëns. Reeves thus belonged to the same uncommon category as Charles Britiffe Smith, Kurtz, Mackinlay and Manning.

Throughout the nineteenth century, Handel was the composer who bulked largest at auctions, which offered a rich field of first and early editions, libretti, and countless items of associated and biographical interest, both from the composer's lifetime and the rest of the eighteenth century. Handel's perennial fascination is seen in such diverse collections as those of the late Earl of Balfour (derived from Julian Marshall and acquired by the National Library of Scotland in 1938), the late T. W. Bourne (presented to the Bodleian), Gerald Coke, Sir Newman Flower, Dr James Hall, Gilbert S. Inglefield and William C. Smith.[1]

Several other specialists were busy on different lines. Percy Scholes was

---

[1] The contents of the last five collections are briefly described by Smith in *Handel. A Descriptive Catalogue of the Early Editions* (London, 1960), pp. xii, xiii, which also gives their holding for each relevant work.

building up two collections for the practical needs of his great contributions to musical history and lexicography. Both were happily preserved intact after his death in 1958. The grand collection of everything relating to Burney and his contemporaries was acquired by James Osborn of Yale University, and the vast assemblage of musical literature and cuttings from journals and newspapers, all supremely well indexed, which was so fruitfully used in the *Oxford Companion to Music*, went to the National Library of Canada in Ottawa.

Gerald Finzi (1901–56) specialised in the study and publication of English orchestral works of the eighteenth century, and to this end acquired many first and early editions of Stanley, Avison, Boyce, Garth, Jackson of Exeter, Felton, Bond, and Mudge. Additions are still being made by his family. The only operatic specialist of this period was Richard Northcott, who served as archivist at Covent Garden from 1906 until his death in 1931. His collection of libretti, letters, documents, illustrations and the like was dispersed: a substantial quantity of the libretti were acquired by the British Museum: letters and association items appeared in Ifan Kyrle Fletcher's catalogue 190, and another batch was sold by Sotheby in May 1959.

The heirs of Stefan Zweig are the only collectors of musical autographs on a large scale who are active in Britain today. The composer best represented is Mozart, of whom they own seventeen compositions, including 'Das Veilchen', five letters and the unique *Verzeichnis aller meiner Werke*. (All these were generously loaned to the British Museum for the Mozart Bicentenary Exhibition of 1956 and are listed in the official catalogue.) For the rest, the heirs of Stefan Zweig possess at least one autograph written by virtually every major composer from J. S. Bach to Richard Strauss, and by many others of secondary interest.

For the last thirty years Arthur Hedley has purposefully collected manuscripts and editions of Chopin's music. He now has eleven works in autograph (including the *trois nouvelles Études*, the E major nocturne, the two polonaises op. 71, and an unpublished waltz in B major of 1848), several early and important copies, some thirty autograph letters, and a large quantity of first editions, especially those of the early works, now very scarce. Hedley acquired most of these treasures (used to such good purpose in his admirable study of the composer) from the collections of Princess Czartoryska and Emma Osborn Pleyel. He also has some fine personal souvenirs of Chopin.

Another collector who pays attention to a single composer is Ronald Stevenson, whose interest in Busoni goes back to 1945. He has amassed some autograph letters, correspondence with the composer's widow and contemporaries, an original pen-drawing of a scene from *Doktor Faust*, a large quantity of printed editions, and much literature about the composer.

A notable example of general collecting on two levels is provided by J. E. Kite, who has amassed over 100 album leaves or small autographs by various composers including Mozart, Verdi, Liszt, Tchaikovsky, Granados, Hahn, Thomas, Cherubini and Massenet, as well as an unpublished piano piece by Elgar. He also has autograph letters by Mendelssohn, Blow, Prokofiev, Haydn, C. P. E. Bach, Borodin and Rimsky-Korsakov. Numerous first editions of Handel, Beethoven, Schumann and Liszt emphasise the catholic value of such a collection.

Alan Tyson has recently begun to specialise in engraved music of the period from about 1760 to 1860, paying as much attention to the textual and musicological value of these editions as to their bibliographical importance. English editions of the classics of this period are his special interest, with particular reference to the light which they may shed on the question of simultaneous publication in England and elsewhere in Europe. While Haydn, Beethoven and Schubert bulk largest, Field, Weber, Clementi, Boccherini and Hummel are also represented in a collection which has reached a total of some 600 items.

Raymond Russell possesses a small but noteworthy collection of works of musical theory and reference, ranging from Adlung, Agricola and Bottrigari to the classics of the late eighteenth century such as Türk and Löhlein, together with other early literature and music related to his special studies on the history of the harpsichord.

Music for the harpsichord has also attracted the interest of C. Vere Pil-kington, who paid special attention to English composers of the eighteenth century, some of whom, such as Aylward and Burton, have been unduly neglected. His collection, which contains some considerable rarities, formed the subject of a paper which he read to the Royal Musical Association in 1957, and which was printed under the title 'A Collection of English 18th century Harpsichord Music' (*Proceedings*, session 83, 1956/57, pp. 89–107).

By far the most extensive specialised collection which has been formed in the twentieth century, and which is still increasing, belongs to Walter N. H. Harding, a British collector active for over fifty years and long resident in America. While he has devoted particular attention to the parallel fields of English and French vocal music of the eighteenth and nineteenth centuries, he has also acquired copies of several editions of *The Dancing Master* from 1686 onwards, to which numerous eighteenth-century collections of country dances form a useful sequel. By way of diversity Harding has collected instructors for the flute and for the voice. His remarkable range of rare English song-books of the seventeenth century is recorded by Day & Mur-rie, who describe it as second only to the holdings of the British Museum. In addition he has some 400 collections of songs composed for the London pleasure gardens. Harding has also amassed over 6000 English sheet-songs, mostly of the periods before 1780, with a strong representation of those issued between 1695 and 1740, supplemented by over 1300 songs taken from eighteenth-century magazines. This extensive group contains a good many Irish imprints. The collection of English sheet-songs is rounded off by some 3500 of a later period, *c.* 1860–1910, representative of the heyday of the music-hall.

Not the least glory of the Harding Collection is the famous assemblage of some 1000 English song-books, dating roughly from 1700 to *c.* 1850, made by Sir John Stainer (d. 1901) and acquired *en bloc* in 1932. This speciality has been strengthened by many important additions of similar books with and without music, illustrated and unillustrated, many being the same work in various editions.

## Trends of the Twentieth Century

The Harding Collection is correspondingly rich in French song-books, which date from 1700 and include a run of the *Chansonnier des graces* from 1797 to 1848. These are complemented by numerous groups from the early and mid eighteenth century—plays with songs, libretti, parodies, and the like, issued for various Parisian theatres. Some 800 octavo sheet-songs, issued between about 1780 and 1830, show a different aspect of the music of France. Its opera is strongly covered by 360 full scores printed before 1815, with an extension into the nineteenth century which comprises some 3000 vocal scores. Further details are given in an article by the collector himself in 'British Song Books and Kindred Subjects' in *The Book Collector* (Winter 1962), pp. 448–59.

We can now pass to the rich harvest of twentieth-century bequests, which can best be presented in an alphabetical sequence of countries and towns. At Cambridge, the music collected by Richard Pendlebury was presented to the Fitzwilliam Museum between 1880 and 1902, and passed to the Faculty of Music in 1925/6. Its historical interest lies chiefly in some now rare orchestral material of the early nineteenth century.

Another notable collector whose generosity enriched the Fitzwilliam Museum was Ralph Griffin (1854–1941), Fellow of St John's, eminent as connoisseur, jurist and judge. Besides the autographs of the two great piano duet-sonatas by Mozart, he gave many autograph letters, a document of 1677 relating to John Blow, and also compositions in autograph by Bach, Storace, Beethoven, S. Wesley and Debussy. Griffin, who collected much else, in his musical interest somewhat resembles Westley Manning. (Griffin also presented music to the Bodleian and the British Museum.) Others who gave music generously to the Fitzwilliam Museum—mainly of the eighteenth and nineteenth centuries—were Squire,[1] E. J. Dent and J. B. Trend.

In 1927 Louis Thompson Rowe bequeathed to King's College his rich collection of eighteenth-century chamber music. In 1930 King's received some 590 volumes from A. H. Mann's library; these were principally in

---

[1] The auction of his library in July 1927 revealed practically no music, but he had presented various manuscripts to the British Museum.

three categories, Handel and Handeliana (including fine libretti), eighteenth-century song-books and some choice early keyboard music. But this was a mere fraction of Mann's collection, about which I may best digress here. He collected books of hymns and psalms on a generous scale: most of them passed to Church House, Westminster, and are now in the British Museum. Many of the early ones bear valuable annotations in his hand, and were well bound by Gray. Ten volumes of autographs by James Hook, containing 128 works, were presented by Mann's family to Cambridge University Library in 1929.[1] Mann's large Crotch collection, and his fifty-four portfolios of manuscript notes relative to East Anglian musicians, were presented to Norwich Public Library.[2] The residue of Mann's music was auctioned in June 1945: besides Tomkins's annotated copy of Morley's *Plaine and Easie Introduction* (which ultimately passed to E. H. W. Meyerstein), and the autograph of Bishop's 'Concertante', he had some good association items and interesting manuscripts of the eighteenth and nineteenth centuries. Mann was indeed a versatile and distinguished collector.

In 1945 Cambridge University Library was enriched by the 486 volumes of music from the seventeenth and eighteenth centuries collected by Franck Thomas Arnold, Lecturer in German at the University College of Monmouth and South Wales. About one quarter of the collection centred upon his monumental study of thorough bass; the remainder comprised much good chamber music, all in admirable condition and finely bound.[3] Another bequest came to the University Library in 1955 from Marion Scott who gave her notable Haydn collection, amounting to 552 items of books, editions, portraits and relics of that composer. It was especially rich in early French editions.[4]

[1] They are now Additional Manuscripts 6632–40.
[2] 'The Crotch Collection. Presented by Bayford Stone Esqre.', *Norwich Public Libraries Readers' Guide*, vol. XII, no. 16 (October/December 1941); and G. A. Stephen, 'Dr Arthur Henry Mann. Memoir and Catalogue of his Manuscripts and Books', *Norwich Public Libraries Readers' Guide*, vol. X, no. 2 (April/June 1930).
[3] See D. R. Wakeling, 'An Interesting Music Collection', *Music & Letters* (July 1945), pp. 159–61; C. L. Cudworth, in the *Cambridge University Reporter* (6 February 1945), pp. 411–16, gives a complete list of the collection.
[4] See *Cambridge University Reporter* (27 July 1955), p. 1660.

I have been unable to discover what happened to the Rev. John Julian's extensive collection of hymns and psalms immediately after his death in 1913. Ultimately it passed to Church House, Westminster, and thence, in 1949, to the British Museum. Though not all the books bear his bold signature, 'J^no Julian', the total cannot, probably, be fewer than 3000 including those books with words only. They are mostly of the nineteenth century, and from nearly every country where printing is known.

Another distinguished collector of psalms and hymns was the Rev. Maurice Frost (d. 1961), who began to assemble these books about 1925, and bequeathed the choicest part of them to the Royal School of Church Music, Addiscombe, Surrey. A wealth of knowledge gained from his collection (which also includes French, German and Dutch rarities) went into his *English & Scottish Psalm & Hymn Tunes, c. 1543–1677* (1953).

Cecil Sharp's lifelong devotion to folk-song led him to amass a remarkable collection relating to it, which he bequeathed in 1924 to the English Folk Dance and Song Society. Over seven hundred items of music and literature are now in the library of Cecil Sharp House, many of the early acquisitions marked with a characteristic bookplate bearing the date 189–, with a space for the last digit to be added. Sharp acquired several of the rare early editions of the *English Dancing Master* and many English and French books on dancing. His manuscripts, not yet old in themselves but containing music of immemorial antiquity, from both Britain and America, were left to the library of his college, Clare.

To the 'Lord Mayor, Aldermen and Citizens of Manchester' Henry Watson gave his great music library of some 16,700 volumes on 24 January 1902 by deed of gift, and continued to look after it until his death in 1911. Besides serving the everyday needs of performance, it contained many rarities —early English music, much of the eighteenth century, and some 400 volumes of theory and (in the true nineteenth-century tradition) some fine old instruments—all described in a recent article[1] by its librarian, L. W. Duck.

[1] 'The Henry Watson Music Library', *Library World* (December 1961), vol. LXIII, pp. 132–6. Watson formally offered his collection in an interesting letter dated 10 October 1899. It is printed in full in the *Manchester Public Free Libraries Quarterly Record* (1899), p. 89.

Of the various collectors who have enriched Oxford, three are of especial historical interest. The Library of the University Music School has received on permanent loan from the Royal College of Music the Terry Bach Collection and the books on the violin amassed by Edward Heron-Allen. C. S. Terry gained world-wide fame from his exhaustive studies of the Bach family, particularly Johann Sebastian and his anglicised son John Christian. Terry was a practical collector who cast his net very wide to cover the biographical, musical and historical background in over 400 volumes. The fruits of Heron-Allen's long acquisitive efforts are, of course, found in his famous publications *De fidiculis bibliographia* and *Opuscula fidicularum*. Some sentences from the preface to section II of his typescript catalogue (a copy of which is in the Music School) deserve quotation: 'It has been my object ever since 1878 to preserve and bind into volumes every scrap of printed matter I could find regarding the violin without any regard for its literary or artistic merit...I commend my volumes of miscellanea to the collector and the historian of the year 2000 A.D.' Besides 'miscellanea' he collected books, pamphlets, novels, stories, dramas and poems relating to the violin. This typescript catalogue, dated 1900, enumerates some 530 volumes. Heron-Allen, a solicitor by profession, and an expert in palmistry, conjuring, Persian literature and *Foraminifera*, added many more before his death in 1943, aged 82. He lavished half-leather bindings, many by Morrell, upon his books and pamphlets, including his privately printed *desiderata* lists. Many volumes bear his bookplates, of which there are three; the first, undated, with his name only; the second, dated 1891, bearing the name of himself and his first wife Marianna, and the third, dated 1925, with his own name again and that of his second wife Edith.

Not the least remarkable Oxford collection is the assemblage of Mendelssohniana begun by Paul Benecke Mendelssohn (a grandson of the composer) and augmented after his death by Margaret Deneke to whom he bequeathed it. (It is deposited on loan in the Bodleian.) Miss Deneke has described the origin of the collection in her booklet, privately printed in 1954, and entitled

*Paul Victor Mendelssohn Benecke, 1868–1944.*[1] The collection comprises autographs, published and unpublished, pocket books of drawings, reports on the pupils of the Leipzig Conservatorium and on the proceedings of the Gewandhaus concerts. There are also some 7000–8000 private letters addressed to Mendelssohn, arranged in twenty-seven volumes, and including autographs from Goethe, Schumann, Wagner and Berlioz. Printed and manuscript music from Mendelssohn's library includes first editions of Chopin and such rarities as the Wittenberg Psalter of 1565.

In Scotland, an equally notable series of bequests testifies to the number of collectors active from about 1860 onwards. W. L. Taylor, a bookseller of Aberdeen, left his collection of psalm versions to the University of that city in 1910. The published catalogue[2] reveals that of the total of some 1700 volumes about two-thirds have music *and* words, the remainder words only, not a few of both categories being rarities of the seventeenth century.

To the National Library of Scotland in 1927 came the famous Glen Collection of some 900 items, mostly of printed Scottish music, and works on that subject. It was amassed by John Glen, a music publisher and dealer and maker of bagpipes, who devoted his life to making the collection, and on the basis of it issued his authoritative books. At his death in 1904 the collection was purchased by Lady Dorothea Ruggles-Brise, and presented by her to the National Library. In 1929 Alexander Wood Inglis, a J.P., and Commissioner of Supply and officer in the Royal Scots Militia, bequeathed his notable library of English and Scottish music of the eighteenth and early nineteenth century, some 740 items in all; and in this same year the National Library also received the Alexander Cowan Collection of over 1000 works of liturgical music, ranging from the sixteenth to the twentieth century. Cowan was a businessman who had long specialised in the subject. In 1952 Cecil Hopkinson gave his splendid Berlioz collection—first and early

---

[1] For further details, see an article by Ernest Walker, 'An Oxford Collection of Mendelssohniana', *Music & Letters*, vol XIX (1938), pp. 426–8

[2] *Catalogue of the Taylor Collection of Psalm Versions* (Aberdeen, 1921). (Aberdeen University Studies, no. 85.)

editions, some autographs, literature and association-pieces—amounting to over 700 items in all. The printed music is described in his monumental bibliography of the composer, published by the Edinburgh Bibliographical Society in 1951.

Of the various collectors who after the time of its foundation have enriched the Reid Music Library in the University of Edinburgh, probably the most influential was Sir Donald Tovey, who was Reid Professor from 1914 onwards. The notable library which he bequeathed in 1940 fairly reflects his remarkable range of activities as a conductor, concert-organiser and writer, especially his famous *Essays in Musical Analysis*.

Glasgow, too, has been the beneficiary of a number of historically important gifts or bequests. H. G. Farmer, a versatile and influential collector, has presented to the University Library two rich collections, one of material relating to Arabic, Persian, Turkish and Jewish music, the other of old Scottish popular music of upwards of 1000 printed items, and has secured a third consisting of about 160 autographs of music by Scottish composers. There were three of these composers—MacCunn, McEwen and Drysdale, to whose autographs were added, in 1949, those of the famous pianist Lamond, which had been acquired by Messrs W. Heffer and Sons from his widow, and were presented by them. A little later, Farmer induced Mrs Lamond to present her husband's collection of programmes, cuttings, drawings of himself and letters (including some from Liszt and Tchaikovsky). In 1930 (also at Farmer's instigation) L. Zavertal gave a miscellaneous collection inherited from V. H. Zavertal and remarkable especially for its Mozart relics.

The most notable addition of music made to Irish libraries during this period came from a British collector associated with Dublin. Ebenezer Prout, still famous for his text-books of musical theory, had been Professor at Trinity College from 1894 to 1909, and when he died in that year his collection was bought for the College by public subscription. The examples in his text-books are drawn from an unusually wide range of music which is to some extent reflected in his collection. It comprises between 1100 and 1200 items, with a good representation of the great masters of the eighteenth and nineteenth centuries. Prout paid a good deal more attention to the lesser composers of the later period than to those of the earlier one.

In 1919 Cardiff Public Libraries received intact the noble collection of music formed by Sir Henry Mackworth (1737–91), of Gnoll Castle, Neath, who was M.P. for Cardiff from 1766 to 1790. After his death, his widow married Mr Capel Hanbury Leigh of Pontypool Park where the collection remained until 1916 when it was sold. The bookseller who bought it offered it to Cardiff Public Libraries, for whom it was secured by R. Bonner Morgan, a Cardiff optician prominent in local musical life. The collection begins with Mace, and ends with the only known copy of John Field's first published work, *c.* 1796. There are in all some 350 pieces, vocal and instrumental, English, French and Spanish songs, Italian operas, English and French chamber music. Sir Henry Mackworth often signed and dated his acquisitions, many of which are of high quality. The names of two other members of his family, Juliana and Robert, also occur.

Another remarkable instance of long preservation was the music of the Filmer family, of Maidstone. The collection was begun by Sir Edward Filmer, a favourite of Queen Elizabeth I, and was continued by his descendants into the early eighteenth century. It comprised some forty manuscripts, mainly of lute and keyboard music, and a dozen printed books of madrigals, nearly all from the press of Vincenti in Venice. It came to light in an attic of the Filmers' ancestral home in 1916, at the death of Sir Robert Filmer. In 1946 the collection was sold to Yale University.[1] The whole history of music-collecting shows that such fortunate survivals as the Mackworth and Filmer music are almost of the same degree of improbability as would be the sight of a pterodactyl flying down Petty Cury.

We may now consider that special class of collectors who would perhaps be more accurately described as 'ghostly' rather than as 'ghosts'. For though we do not at present know the full extent and scope of their libraries of music, we do know that they existed and that most of them did collect.

---

[1] See Brooks Shepherd, Jr., 'A Repertory of 17th Century English House Music', *Journal of the American Musicological Society*, vol. IX, no. 1 (1956), p. 61.

It would have been almost impertinent to categorise Bever and Hawkins as 'ghosts', for though no catalogues of their collections are extant, we know a good deal about their tastes and specialities. But with others it is different, for the evidence is often slender. How far can an occasional mention in a sale-catalogue, or a signed title-page be taken as proof of zealous collecting? On the title-page of the Burney sale-catalogue we read: '...a rare collection of the most choice madrigals, many of which were from the D'Arcy and Gostling collections.' Gostling we have met: but who, of the ancient and exceedingly numerous family of D'Arcy, was he who collected madrigals? We have a clue from the title-pages of a number of English part-books in the British Museum[1] which bear the signature 'Conyers D'Arcy'. The only member of the family then so named was the son of Elizabeth Conyers and Thomas D'Arcy who in 1605 became Conyers, seventh Lord D'Arcy de Knayth and fourth Lord Conyers. But whether he collected other music besides English, I have failed to discover. James Matthew owned his copy of Yonge's *Musica Transalpina* which included other madrigals in d'Arcy's hand.

Again, Humphrey Wanley owned a copy of the very scarce 1638 edition of the famous Dutch song-book *Bellerophon*[2] and three very varied musical manuscripts now in the Harleian Collection. Wanley acquired his *Bellerophon* on 13 February 1696/7, at the time when he was working at the Bodleian and was sometimes in company with Dean Aldrich;[3] but having found no other evidence, even in his correspondence with Tudway, that he had any real musical interests, I must reluctantly rank him with Lumley and Heber, and not as a true music collector. Similarly, although David Garrick had a little music among his large general library as catalogued for the sale of 1823[4] and though he knew Burney well, he must be left in the class of general book-collectors.

---

[1] The earliest is Morley's *First Book of Balletts* of 1595. Tenbury MS. 309 also bears D'Arcy's signature.
[2] Crotch sale, no. 182; in two anonymous sales, 29 April 1873, lot 181 (S.C.P. 155 (10) and 20 July 1873, lot 128 S.C.P. 157 (7)): and later in the Cummings sale, lot 274.
[3] Hiscock, *op. cit.* p. 36.
[4] Including a Zarlino *Opere* (1589), later in S.C.P. 85 (2), lot 163.

# Trends of the Twentieth Century

The admirable indexes of Hughes-Hughes's three-volume catalogue are full of the names of those who owned a few manuscripts, but I have doubts about the status of many of them. In sale-catalogues we find passing mention of eminent musicians who had owned a choice item—such as William Child (d. 1697), John Keeble (d. 1786), pupil of Kelway and Pepusch, and Thomas Chilcot (d. 1766)—but here too I have doubts.

On the other hand, the name of James Kent (1700–76) successively organist of Trinity College, Cambridge, and of Winchester Cathedral, appears so frequently that I think he may have collected systematically, principally English church music of a generation earlier than his own. The Royal Music Library contains some good manuscripts that bear his name. I have tried, in vain, to find out who was Henry Hase, also well represented in the Royal Music Library and in the Royal College manuscripts and frequently named by the auctioneers (e.g. at the Shoubridge and Warren sales). He was not a university graduate, but bore a coat of arms (as witness his bookplate in the Franks Collection). His interest seems to have lain chiefly in Italian music of the seventeenth century. One of his treasures was a manuscript of Legrenzi's unpublished opera *La Divisione del mondo*.[1]

The famous singer Venanzio Rauzzini, who died at Bath in 1810, was certainly a collector. The sale of his library was conducted by Mrs Plura on 26 December 1810 at 2 Gay Street, Bath,[2] but no copy of the catalogue survives. Clementi possibly had an outstanding collection: two items of mid eighteenth-century Italian theory in the Horsley sale (lots 154–65) are stated to be his. That a sale of his library did take place is attested by Sarah Emett in a letter[3] relating to the autograph of book 2 of Bach's 'Forty-eight' but what other music it comprised we do not know. Since, however, his household once included a maidservant who used some of his autographs to light a fire, anything may have happened to the bulk of his collection.

---

[1] Shoubridge sale, 30 June 1873 (S.C.P. 156 (12), lot 263).

[2] Information from an advertisement in *The Bath Chronicle*, 13 and 20 December 1810. The Ellerton sale-catalogue and the Warren (autograph) catalogue mention what is apparently another sale of 1811, the latter specifying 6 March.

[3] Bound up with B.M. Add. MS. 35022.

The first Earl Cawdor and his wife Elizabeth had some enthusiasm for Jomelli and his contemporaries. Their respective signatures occur on a number of manuscripts in the Royal Music.[1] Other items from the Cawdor Collection appeared in the Bennett sale.[2]

In the Taylor sale of 1863 there is listed a sale-catalogue of the collection of 'T. Vaughan', presumably the minor composer Thomas Vaughan who died in 1843: the sole copy extant seems to be that in the Harding Collection. The Bennett sale-catalogue mentions the sale of Cipriani Potter's library (probably a sound working collection), and this too is otherwise almost unknown.[3] Lonsdale possessed an 'Ashley' sale-catalogue of 1813; where is it now? Without it, we cannot tell which of the numerous Ashley family of musicians this was. Occasionally *The Harmonicon* gives valuable information about 'ghosts', as when it mentions[4] the disposal of the libraries of two distinguished organists, Benjamin Jacobs (to whom Samuel Wesley addressed his famous letters on Bach) and Mathew Cooke, organist of St George's, Bloomsbury, which were both auctioned by Musgrave on 3–5 March 1830.

Perhaps one of the most tantalising of all these 'ghosts' is the well-known musical writer John Bishop of Cheltenham (d. 1890) whose large library is mentioned with deserved respect by Squire in *Grove*.[5] During Bishop's lifetime a 'Descriptive Catalogue' was issued *c.* 1885, which shows it to have been rich in books about instruments and theory. No sale is known, and, not unexpectedly, the collection bore little relation to the *Repertorium musicae antiquae* which Bishop published in collaboration with Warren as early as 1848. Intended to cover the early German and Italian masters, it was based mostly on the latter's collection.

It is Warren's autograph catalogue of his own library that provides an

[1] That this was the first and not the second Earl can be proved by comparison with those letters which, when Harleian Trustee from 1834 to 1860, he wrote to Sir Frederic Madden.

[2] See also J. R. Sterndale Bennett, *The Life of William Sterndale Bennett* (Cambridge, 1907), p. 278: 'The Earl [of Cawdor] had valuable scores of Bach's works in his library, and...sent some of them to Bennett as a present.' The Earl was a friend of the Prince Consort, and a patron of the Bach Society.

[3] A volume of J. S. Bach in the British Museum, bound in half green morocco, bears Potter's name on a label on the front cover.

[4] 1830, pp. 136, 179, with some details of contents and prices.

[5] First edition, s.v. 'Musical Libraries', vol. II, p. 423.

important source about some 'lost' collectors dating from the seventeen-nineties onwards. He owned over 100 sale-catalogues, and wrote the owners' names and the dates of sale on pages 229–234 of his personal catalogue. We find there fourteen names not in the British Museum's *List* of 1915, as follows: Paul Stobler (18, 19 May 1795); F. Barthélemon (9 February 1809); J. C. Flack (24 June 1813); Daniel Walker (21 June 1810); John Bacon (26 June 1816); Mr Guise (8 June 1807); T. Jones of Nottingham (13–15 February 1826); W. Monck Mason (30 January 1834); George Cooper (Assistant Organist of St Paul's); E. A. Kellner, teacher to George IV, and Mrs Fawcett (all three on 9 December 1844); Barham Livius (5 February 1845); Benjamin Cooke (5, 6 August 1845); George Penson (9 March 1847).

Warren's sale-catalogues were bound in five volumes of which vol. 1, containing those dated before 1838, is now lost. Vols. 2, 3, 4 and 5 however, ranging up to 1853, are now in the Harding Collection, which thus contains the details of the music owned by the last eight collectors in the above list. (It may be mentioned that the Cooke sale of 1845 contained—lot 316—an 'autograph' of John Bull containing fantasies and pavans in tablature.)

To this roll of names, famous and obscure, should be added those of whom I have made passing mention in my previous lectures. Seen through the mists of time, all these shadowy figures stand on the distant bank of the great river of collecting and seem to stretch out their hands 'ripae ulterioris amore'. We must hope that future research, fortified by a modicum of luck, will aid them to cross the flood and so to join the throng of those whose collections are known in luminous detail, to the enrichment of our knowledge of this venerable tradition.

From 'ghosts' let us now turn to more palpable objects—the prices which collectors paid for their music. This is, of course, a vast subject and though I have alluded to a few individual prices, to assemble more of this data for deductive and historical purposes is rather in the nature of an *excursus* from the proper subject of these lectures. All I can hope to offer is a summary, first for printed music and then for manuscripts. The publishers' selling prices of music are known from the late seventeenth century onwards, from a few surviving trade catalogues. The most notable is a sale (not auction) of *c.* 1690, at which Henry Playford offered cheap 121 items, principally English, of the early and mid seventeenth century.[1] The early auction prices do not generally show a very great increase on the original cost, but the earliest extant records only date from the later eighteenth century. (It is a great pity that Hawkins did not record the prices at the Britton sale.) Here we meet a difficulty, in the case of printed music, because for some time very few items were catalogued separately, and it is impossible to deduce the cost of one item from the price paid for a lot including six concertos and six symphonies, or six sets of madrigals. But in such sales as those of Boyce and Horne, one guinea or 25s. is a fair price for any one of such lots.

It was not until well into the nineteenth century that reference books were compiled which gave some criteria of scarcity and so began to affect prices. Even then, we have little idea of the true competitive demand. The names in the priced catalogues are those of both dealers and collectors: the former were on the whole more numerous. American competition for music hardly makes itself felt until the eighteen-nineties and until about the same time the influence of Continental buyers seems to have been small. But even with all these slightly uncertain factors, prices of music must have been affected by the value of money and economic conditions to much the same extent as were the prices of books.

We can however get a fairly clear picture of the fluctuation of prices by studying the recurrence of the same works or of nearly comparable ones, from the early nineteenth century onwards. Obviously, the most frequently recurring items will be those published in England. Morley's *Plaine and Easie Introduction* (1597) turns up with the amiable regularity of certain gentlemen who can be seen and heard in front of the Tavern at Lord's on a warm afternoon. In 1811 (Compton) it fetched 10s.; in 1813, lacking title (R. Smith), 2s. 6d.; in 1849 (Sir Giffin Wilson), £2—this was James Kent's

[1] Copies of the catalogue are in the Bodleian (Wood. E. 22 (9)) and in the British Museum (Bagford, Harl. 5936/419, 420).

copy, apparently perfect; in 1850 Cummings paid £1. 2s. for a copy at the Scott sale; in 1858 Allott's copy fetched 8s. 6d.; in 1860 Smart's made only 5s.; by 1934 Stainer's copy fetched £17. 10s. Now a copy is knocked down at about £50.

Let us take another hardy annual, Arnold's edition of Handel. In 1799 Horne's copy of the first 170 numbers made £15. 15s. Robert Smith owned two copies, both handsomely bound, and selected for him by Dr Arnold. These, in 1813, made £45. 3s. and £46. 4s. respectively. Never again before 1900 do we find such high prices. An outline of the sequence is this: 1813 (a professor) £22. 1s.; 1832 (Groombridge) £18. 18s.; 1847 (Lady Sykes) £12. 0s.; 1848 (Picart) £16. 16s.; 1849 (Wilson) £13; 1850 (Scott) £3. 15s.; 1850 (Duke of Cambridge, large paper) £19, paid by Lord Falmouth; 1851 (Street) £8; 1852 (Stafford Smith) £7. 7s.; 1858 (Allott: Dr Bever's copy) £7. 5s.; 1861 (Perkins) £5. 5s.; 1862 (Horsley, bought by Prout) £3. 7s.; 1863 (Chichester) £10; 1863 (Taylor) £4. 12s. 6d.; and so on. The lower of these prices were influenced by slight imperfections: complete sets rarely occur. Other Handel items were rather more steady. Walsh and Cluer editions always seem to have commanded fair prices. For instance at the Baker sale of 1855, forty of them together made £72.

Another touchstone is afforded by English madrigals and other publications of the late sixteenth and early seventeenth century. In the early eighteen-hundreds, a lot comprising six sets of parts made a guinea or 25s. The Musical Antiquarian Society's activity in the eighteen-forties probably helped prices to rise. At an anonymous sale of 1864[1] there were seventeen lots of such works, all complete. The average price was £15 per set. Yet in 1863 at the Gauntlett sale the two sets of Wilbye's Madrigals fetched only £2. 17s. and £2. 3s. At the Sykes sale of 1847 Byrd's *Psalmes, Sonets* (1588) brought £1. 3s. For madrigals and the like, £20 was an average price for a complete set up to about 1918, when in the Littleton sale, Watson's madrigals (1590) fetched £46. Then came the Christie-Miller sale of 1919, which, mainly because of the presence of the American dealer George D. Smith,

[1] S.C.P. 95 (6).

more than trebled most prices—Adson's *Courtly masquing Ayres*, £84; Campion's *Two Bookes of Ayres*, £190; Dowland's *Third and last Booke of Songs*, £280; Peerson, *Grave Chamber Musique*, £290; Morley's *Madrigals* (1594), £98; his four-voice *Canzonets*, £92; his two-voice *Canzonets*, £66; Damon's *Former Booke* and *Second Booke*, together £250. But in the 'twenties sanity returned, and the average price of madrigals, at any rate, as shown in the Willmott and Arkwright sales of 1935 and 1939, was much nearer £40, which is now, I suppose, about the average price per single part.

If Allison's *Psalms* (1599) made only 1s. at the Parker sale of 1813, it seems absurd that the 1721 edition of *Orpheus Britannicus* from the same collection went at £14. 14s. Perhaps this is no less illogical than the 6s. made in 1852 by Stafford Smith's copy of Purcell's *Ode to St Cecilia*, or than the 6d. fetched in 1832 by the younger Hawkins's copy of Banister & Low's *Ayres and Dialogues* (1678). By this standard, the 11s. paid in 1867 for Bates's copy of Dowland's *Micrologus* (1608) seems quite expensive. As late as 1879 Cummings paid only £1. 6s. for Snoxell's copy of the Lawes brothers' *Choice Psalms* of 1648. I have already mentioned the remarkably low prices paid for some great English rarities by Thorpe at the Jones sale of 1825. To give one more English example—at the Dowding sale of 1823 the Cianchettini & Sperati edition of symphonies by Haydn, Mozart and Beethoven was noted as scarce, barely twelve years after production. The Duke of Sussex's copy fetched £2. 10s. in 1846, the Wilson copy £2. 3s. in 1859 and the Dent copy £110 in 1958.

Some foreign prices show a broadly similar pattern. In 1847 Gauntlett's copies of some rare early theory went as follows: Diruta's *Il Transilvano*, £1. 13s.; Gafori's *Practica musicae* (1512), £1. 10s.; Salinas's *De musica libri VII* (once Pepusch's), £1. 14s.; similarly, in 1865 twenty-three parts of various works printed by LeRoy and Ballard made £1. In 1884 Hullah's copies of Wollick's *Opus aureum* and Reuchlin's *Scenica progymnasmata* made, respectively, £2. 2s. and £1. 3s. In 1876 a copy of Frosch's *Rerum musicarum opusculum* sold for 17s. Yet in 1939 Arkwright's copy of Philips's *Libro primo de madrigali* (Phalèse, 1596), four of the five parts, fetched but

£4. 10s. In 1867 Bates's copy of Caroso's *Il Ballarino*, together with a quantity of French early seventeenth-century music, made but £2. 2s.

Seventeenth-century works were in about proportionate demand. Wanley's copy of *Bellerophon* made 7s. at the first of its three appearances in 1873, 8s. at its second and 15s. in the Cummings sale. Husk bought five of the six parts of the collection *De' fiori del giardino* (Nürnberg, 1604) for £1. 5s. From Scott's library in 1850 Galilei's *Dialogo* (1602) made 2s. Ayrton's copies of *Euridice* and *Le Nuove musiche*, bound together, fetched £4. 12s.; Bates's thirty-five parts of various Masses and *Cantiones sacrae* by Praetorius sold for £1. 10s. in 1867; Ouseley paid £1. 10s. for Engel's copy of Finger's *Sonatae xii* (1688). In 1877, at G. T. Smith's sale, three of the four parts of Le Jeune's *Cent cinquante pseaumes* (1650) sold for 18s.

The great German complete editions issued from mid nineteenth century onwards hardly come into consideration, but it is worth noting, wistfully, that in 1888 at a mixed sale[1] Trubner secured all twenty-four series of the Breitkopf Mozart for £7. 10s.

The changing values of manuscript music are rather less easy to define than those of printed items of relative interest and importance. One and the same manuscript is probably not often offered for sale: sometimes, it appears only once, then goes abroad, or into the hands of a long-lived collector who presents it to an institutional library. Nevertheless, noting the prices of representative manuscripts of different schools and periods, we can get a fair idea of their gradual rise from what seems absurdly cheap in the late eighteenth and mid nineteenth century to the general inflation of our own times.

Virginal music was long in small demand. The Cosyn Book fetched but £1. 2s. at the Boyce sale. And her volume, once wrongly described as the property of King Philip and Queen Mary,[2] was sold at Picart's sale in 1848 for £1. 1s. The Mulliner Book was offered for £6. 6s. by Hamilton in 1845; at Rimbault's sale in 1877 it was bought for £82 by Cummings, and was acquired from him at that price by the British Museum. In 1866[3] Quaritch

---

[1] S.C.P. 239 (1).      [2] Now B.M. Add. MS. 31392.
[3] Lot 173, anonymous sale, 2 March, S.C.P. 105 (7).

bought an Elizabethan tablature of pavans, allemands and the like for £1. 18s.

Early copies of madrigals were almost two a penny. Oliphant paid only 3s. 6d. in 1861 for a complete set from the time of James I.[1] Sacred music seems to have been more prized. Ouseley bought a collection of 165 full and verse anthems, from the collection of W. J. Porter of Canterbury, for £11 at an anonymous sale of 1872.[2] An association-piece could also command a rather high price. Halliwell had to pay £4. 2s. 6d. for a manuscript copy,[3] probably in Playford's autograph, of all four parts of his *Collection of Songs and Glees*, now in the Euing Library. Perhaps this was because the fly-leaf of the bass part bore a list of the members of the Musical Club in the Old Jewry to whom Playford dedicated his *Musical Companion* of 1667. Nor was the seventeenth-century instrumental music in manuscript much more in demand, for a long time. At the Aylesford sale in 1918, £2. 12s. was sufficient to secure an early manuscript of Baltzar's violin sonatas. For a slightly later item, S. L. Weiss's autograph collection of lute preludes and other pieces, written *c.* 1718, Ouseley paid but £1. 7s.[4] The dealer Whittingham gave only 5s. 6d. for an early manuscript of toccatas by Pasquini, Poglietti and Kerll, from the Stafford Smith Collection.[5]

Though the autograph of the twelve Sinfonie by Alessandro Scarlatti cost the Privy Purse but £4. 11s. at the Boyce sale in 1777, this was quite a high price for that date, and suggests how prized that composer then was. In 1872 at the third Warren sale, twenty autograph Scarlatti cantatas fetched only £3. 5s. Handel, because of the great concentration in the Royal Music Library, has always been scarce and has usually fetched good prices. But it is a far cry from the now lost *Amadigi* autograph, which Marshall bought at the Smee sale in 1879 for £35, to the £1800 paid at Sotheby's in 1954 for four leaves comprising four songs to Spanish and French words. As a

---

[1] Lot 431, anonymous sale, 6 September 1861, S.C.P. 77 (6).
[2] Lot 355, 28 October, S.C.P. 152 (3).
[3] Lot 179, anonymous sale, 2 March 1866, S.C.P. 105 (7).
[4] Lot 307, anonymous sale, 29 April 1863, S.C.P. 86 (9). It is now B.M. Add. 30387.
[5] Lot 441, anonymous sale, 6 September 1861, S.C.P. 77 (6).

milestone on the way, let us note the £500 paid at a sale in 1937 for the four leaves containing the final chorus from the autograph of *Floridante*. Squire was both shrewd and fortunate when he bought the pieces for a musical clock in a unique manuscript copy for £2. 6s. at the Aylesford sale in 1918 and added them to the Royal Music. But we should remember that at the Bates sale of 1867 a duett and trio by Handel, stated to be in his autograph and from the collections of Bartleman, Bever and Thomas Norris, had fetched but 1s.

At his infrequent appearances, Haydn seems to have been a drug on the nineteenth-century market. At the Ayrton sale of 1858, forty pages of the autograph of *Armida* made only £1. 3s., being probably the missing portion of the autograph as previously sold (1853) from the Falmouth Collection for £5. 5s., and now in the Royal College of Music. There was a good deal more Mozart about, mostly from the Stumpff sale of 1847 onwards. On that occasion, the total for forty-two autographs of piano and chamber music, including the 'great' quartets, was £34, an average of less than 31s. per work. Of the Stumpff items which came on the English market again in the next few decades, that of the Fugue in C minor fetched £12. 10s. (Boone) at the Warren sale of 23 May 1872, and the String Quintet in D ultimately passed into the Smee Collection whence it was sold in 1879 to G. B. Davy for £45. Again, in the Ayrton sale, the autograph of the Clarinet Trio (K. 498) fetched £3. 3s., and then went to France. Considerably later, when A. G. Kurtz's collection was sold in 1895, the autograph of the A minor Rondo went for £28 and that of the variations on 'La bergère Celimène' for £33. 12s. (The latter was from the Stumpff Collection.) In 1924, at the Bridge sale, the manuscript of Attwood's exercises, written under Mozart's supervision with many corrections, annotations and two compositions in his hand, made £110. In 1935, the autograph of 'Das Veilchen' in the Speyer Collection was valued by Haas at £800. A remarkable example of increased value is afforded by the manuscript of the earliest known compositions of the infant Mozart which his father wrote out on two leaves in 1761. In 1954 they were auctioned for £95: in 1960 they reappeared in Catalogue 40 of the Scientific Library Service, New York, for $9500.

Beethoven, though relatively few autographs have been owned by British collectors, has always fetched fairly high prices. In 1879 Marshall paid £55 for sixty-one leaves of an autograph containing sketches of the Pastoral Symphony and other works.[1] In 1958 four leaves of sketches of the Sonata op. 106 fetched £3700, which suggests what a collector would have to pay for the autograph of the complete sonata if ever it were to come on the market. In 1935 the proof sheets of the Archduke Trio, then in the Speyer Collection, were valued at £60. At auction in 1960 they fetched £2750, which almost brings Beethoven into the same range of increase as Caxton and Picasso, though not perhaps into that of the Bay Psalm Book.

Mendelssohn has always commanded fairly high prices, whether for association items or autographs. For instance, at the Bennett sale of 1875, Taphouse paid £52 for the autograph of the full score of the 'Fingal's Cave' overture and £62 for thirteen autograph letters written to the publisher Coventry. In 1872 a manuscript first violin part of *Elijah*, 'the first brought into England and used at the first performance at the Birmingham Festival' with Mendelssohn's alterations and corrections, was purchased by W. Mason for £6. 15s.[2] A study of the recurrence of autographs by such composers as Elgar or Brahms would reveal broadly the same tendency within a shorter, more recent period. It is perhaps difficult to make much sense of all this, but allowing for the changing value of money, a few deductions can be attempted from the rather haphazard selection of prices over the last century and a half: first, auction prices have often proved as unpredictable in the past as they are now; second, they have always been influenced by the nature of the occasion and the reputation of those bidding; third, the phenomenal rise in these prices during the last twenty years has still not caught up with the rise in the prices of books and manuscripts in

---

[1] Fuchs sale, 23 April, lot 110: acquired by the British Museum in 1880 as Add. MS. 31766.
[2] Lot 327, anonymous sale, 26 March, S.C.P. 148 (1).

general. The astute collector can still occasionally buy some music for less than £10 which he could sell for well over £1000.

Now, as we enter the sixth decade of the twentieth century, the scale of the map that I described at the outset has, I hope, been enlarged and many of its details clarified. The pageant which (if at last I may combine my two metaphors) has wound its way across this terrain, from the days of William Heather to those of the heirs of Stefan Zweig, has faded, and the stage is strangely empty. Yet, despite the sad ghosts that have hovered at times along its path, this pageant has been by no means insubstantial. Indeed, its very richness prompts the question 'what of the future?'.

The statistics for auctions that I have given at intervals during these lectures point unmistakably to the writing on the wall. For in the collecting of music we are surely they 'whose generations are ordained in this setting part of time'. Where are the mid twentieth-century equivalents of Lord Fitzwilliam, of Bartleman and Edward Jones, of Ouseley and Rimbault, of Marshall and Cummings? Their like does not exist and never will exist again. New collectors will of course continue to come to the fore but they will not be numerous, and they will tend more and more to specialise. Their field is bound to be limited to the period from about 1720 onwards. For the supply of important manuscripts and of great rarities of printed music, so abundant in earlier times, is now almost exhausted; nearly all have passed into institutional libraries. Even, therefore, over fifty years or more, and given all the necessary resources, a general collection on the grand scale achieved by the giants of the nineteenth century simply cannot now be assembled.

We should therefore be all the more thankful that the great collectors of the past made such splendid use of their opportunities. True, time and reformers have torn sad gaps in the fabric of our musical heritage, but from the mid sixteenth century onwards the proportion of survival borders increasingly on the miraculous—all the more so when we reflect on the hard use that unbound music habitually receives—thrust into pockets, stacked on music desks, or often projecting awkwardly from shelves of inadequate depth. It sometimes seems as if Clio herself—and Clio, remember, was the muse of lyre-playing no less than of history—had inspired the efforts of the collectors, who could thus invoke her by name—

O vetustatis veneranda custos,
     aurea Clio,
tu nihil magnum sinis interire,
nil mori clarum pateris, reservans
posteris prisci monumenta saecli
     condita libris.

In these prophetic lines of Phocas, let us pay a final tribute to the magnificent work of conservation which twelve generations of British collectors have achieved by their devotion to books of music. For without their zeal our knowledge of musical palaeography and bibliography, the study of musical history and the scholarly editing of music for performance, indeed the whole basis of our musical culture, would all have been immeasurably poorer than they are today.

# APPENDIX A

# THE ROYAL MUSIC LIBRARY AND ITS COLLECTORS

The first of the two articles forming this appendix originally appeared in *The Book Collector*, Autumn 1958, as a piece of some topical interest. It raised a problem of identity (p. 108) which could not be solved in the time then available. In a second article (*The Book Collector*, Winter 1960), I was able to publish the solution, which was of such a kind that it has proved impracticable to merge the two articles into one for the present volume. I have therefore reprinted them separately in their original sequence, with some changes and additions.

## 1. THE GROWTH OF THE COLLECTION

It was in March 1911, barely ten months after King George V's accession to the throne, that he greatly enriched the world of musical learning by depositing the 'King's Music Library' (as it was later officially known for a time) on loan in the British Museum. The officer most closely connected with the deposit was William Barclay Squire, then Assistant Keeper (later Deputy Keeper) in charge of the Music Room. After his retirement in 1920, Squire devoted all his energy to cataloguing the royal collection, of which he was appointed the first Honorary Curator in 1923. Without a catalogue, the bulk of the collection still remained unknown and difficult to consult, and by the terms of the deposit, the Trustees were required to publish one 'as soon as conveniently possible'. The catalogue was ultimately printed in an edition of 500 copies.

Part I, devoted to the Handel manuscripts, appeared in 1927, the year of Squire's much regretted death. He had been able to complete this volume, with the generously acknowledged help of a few specialists, and had laid down the lines to be followed for the remainder. Part II, *The Miscellaneous Manuscripts* (1929) was by Hilda Andrews; Part III, *Printed Music and Musical Literature* (1929) had been begun by Squire, and was completed by

William C. Smith, his successor in the Music Room. Since it was Squire who had been largely instrumental in securing the deposit of the Royal Music Library[1] its catalogue was in every sense, as the preface to Part I says, 'the final monument of his many services to musical history'.

Thus, in brief, was this great collection made publicly available. It became the actual property of the nation on 27 November 1957, when Her Majesty Queen Elizabeth II was graciously pleased to announce that the original loan was converted into an outright presentation to the Trustees of the British Museum. This munificent gift was made to mark the bicentenary of the presentation of the Old Royal Library to the British Museum. Before 1911, only a few specialists had been granted access to the collection of music within Buckingham Palace: after that date, and especially from 1929 onwards, its richness as a musicological source became far more widely appreciated. But no study has ever been devoted to its bibliographical interest. This is so varied that this article must be confined to the growth of the Library in terms of important single items or small collections which have a definite association with a member of the royal house, or with some person of musical distinction in their service. The number of volumes so associable is relatively small. The visible evidence consists of armorial bearings, initials on bindings, autograph signatures and manuscript notes, bookplates and stamps. In some cases ownership can be established from external sources, but apart from a few hundred volumes thus identifiable, there is a large residue of which the provenance is only conjectural or quite obscure.

Broadly speaking, it is the private, domestic musical interests of some ten generations of English royalty which can be seen in the collection: not until the nineteenth century was it substantially enlarged by the fruits of their public patronage of festivals, concerts and the like, and by gifts from various sources. Very few of the books have any connection with the use of music as an essential part of State ceremony. The two earliest volumes, *Souter Liedekēs...op alle die Psalmen vā David*, printed by Symm Cock at Antwerp

---

[1] See A. Hyatt King, 'William Barclay Squire, 1855–1927', *The Library*, vol. XII (March 1957), pp. 1–10.

in 1540, and the manuscript anthology compiled from *c.* 1580 onwards by John Baldwin, a Gentleman of the Chapel Royal, bear no marks of provenance or acquisition. They may have been acquired long after the time of their origin (as were probably many other books of the sixteenth and seventeenth centuries), in some cases two hundred years later. A definite provenance can first be established early in the seventeenth century when King Charles I had his arms impressed on the fine binding of a manuscript containing twenty-three sets of fantasies, possibly autograph, by Giovanni Coperario (born as John Cooper). This italianised Englishman, who died in 1626, had been music-master to the children of James I, and it is known from Playford[1] that Charles I was especially fond of 'those incomparable Phantasies of Mr. Coperario to the Organ'.

There is no certain trace of any books added by the later Stuarts, but under the Hanoverians the collection grew rapidly. What may be termed its 'Handelian era' seems to have begun not long after Handel arrived in England, towards the end of 1710. During the second decade of the century, the precise nature of his relationship with the royal family is uncertain, and the evidence is conflicting; but it seems fairly certain that from about 1720 onwards he taught music to one or more of the daughters of George I, and held a salaried post from 1727 onwards.[2] Whatever Handel's position, his printed music bulks large in the royal collection, the earliest item being the score of *Rinaldo* published in 1711.

Four years after Handel arrived in London, King George I came to the throne, and it seems very likely—to put the possibility no higher—that he brought with him from Hanover[3] some part of the fine collection of the operas and other vocal works by Agostino Steffani and other composers. Steffani was a remarkable man, who took Holy orders in 1680, and became Court Composer to the Elector of Hanover shortly after 1689; he had

[1] *Introduction to the Skill of Music* (London, 1687), and later editions, preface, A7ᵛ.
[2] See William C. Smith, *Concerning Handel* (London, 1948), pp. 32, 40–2, 51–3.
[3] This is stated categorically, though without reference to any authority, by W. G. Cusins, in his fine article on Steffani in Grove, *Dictionary of Music and Musicians* (London, 1st ed., 1890), vol. III, p. 697. This statement was repeated in 1920 by Squire in a memorandum submitted to the Trustees of the British Museum.

found time in a busy musical life to undertake several diplomatic missions for the Pope. When in Rome in 1708–9, he met Handel. For his services he was created Bishop (*in partibus infidelium*) of Spiga in Anatolia—a rare distinction for a musician.

Although the manuscripts from Hanover became the property of George I, if only by apparent right of importation, evidence has recently come to light which shows that in the next generation the ownership of part of them passed to Queen Caroline. She has hitherto been identified in the Royal Music only by her arms on the bindings of a few volumes (mostly Handel), but in 1961 there was discovered at Windsor Castle a manuscript catalogue of which the title-page reads: *A Catalogue of the Royal Library of her late Majesty Queen Caroline. Distributed into Faculties. 1743.* One interesting feature of this catalogue is that it gives a shelf-mark for each book. None however is found in her music, even in volumes still in the original binding.

Her music-books occupy the pages numbered 175–7 and part of an un-numbered page in this volume. Page 177 is headed 'Musick in Mst. Musica per il Theatro d'Hannover', and contains thirty-one items, most of which can still be identified. Her printed music (pages 175, 176) comprises twenty-eight volumes, containing thirty pieces, of which however barely half are in the Royal Music today. The earliest imprint is Scaletta's *Scala di musica* (Rome, 1685). The Queen's musical interests seem to have been fairly catholic, for she owned some French ballets, cantatas and dance music, Dutch, English and German hymn-books, and works by Purcell, Clayton and Ariosti. Handel, rather curiously, is represented only by one work, the score of *Otho*.

Yet as the Royal Music grew in the course of the century, it was Handel who by choice or accident bulked larger than any other composer. Most of his major works, right down to the great Arnold edition of 1787–97, are here and royal names appear regularly in the subscription lists. It is not impossible that some early works were presented by Handel himself.

Some important manuscript copies of his music were added during his life, and more in the seventeen-sixties and early seventeen-seventies.[1] The supreme return for royal patronage came between 1772 and 1774 when the incomparable collection of autographs (now bound in ninety-seven volumes) was given to George III by John Christopher Smith the younger. This Smith, the son of Handel's amanuensis, was a member of the household of Augusta, Dowager Princess of Wales[2] and had received from her a salary of £200 a year. When, on her death, George III continued this payment as a life pension, Smith gave His Majesty the Handel autographs as a mark of gratitude. Seldom can royal generosity have reaped so rich a musical reward.[3] The value and balance of the Handel collection was enhanced by later accessions, notably the manuscripts which Barclay Squire purchased in 1918 at the sale of the library of the Earl of Aylesford (a descendant of Charles Jennens, one of Handel's oratorio librettists) and added by permission.

Handel, although the most eminent, was only one of a number of composers with Court appointments whose music came into the royal collection in the course of the century. C. F. Abel, who was chamber musician to Queen Charlotte in *c.* 1765, is represented by numerous chamber and orchestral works, many with finely engraved dedications to royalty and to the nobility. His close friend John Christian Bach is likewise represented by many English and some French editions. More interesting, however, are his manuscripts, including eight autographs, three of which were the property of Queen Charlotte, whose music teacher Bach was from 1763 onwards.[4] Another manuscript, containing the dances used at the Court Balls from 1761 to 1787, is in the hand of C. F. Weidemann, who taught the flute

---

[1] Two volumes of a set of anthems, mostly in the hand of the elder Smith and bound almost identically with those in the royal collection, were apparently given away by King George III. They ultimately passed into the library of Novello & Co. who have recently deposited them in the British Museum on loan.

[2] The only book that is identifiable as having belonged to the Princess Augusta is a copy of *Amaryllis* (London, *c.* 1750) one of the most delightful of all the illustrated song-books of the eighteenth century. Its charming binding bears her name in a panel on the cover of each volume.

[3] See [William Coxe] *Anecdotes of George Frederick Handel and John Christopher Smith* (London, 1799), pp. 49, 52–5, pt. 2: this seems to be the earliest account of the gift.

[4] Some of the manuscripts may have been presented by Bach's widow to the Queen who, after his death in 1782, gave her a pension and money for the journey back to her native Italy.

to George III[1] and was conductor of the King's band. It was, apparently, through Weidemann that the collection received a nearly contemporary copy of Handel's earliest surviving work, a set of six sonatas for two oboes and bass, composed *c.* 1696, for which this manuscript is the sole source.

Here it is appropriate to say more of Queen Charlotte's enthusiasm for music, which was perhaps even greater than her husband's. She was pleased to accept the dedication of the Sonatas, op. 3 (K.10–15) which Mozart offered to her on 18 January 1765, nine days before his ninth birthday. The copy presented is splendidly bound in red morocco, and includes a separate violin part in the hand of Mozart's father, Leopold. In 1788 Queen Charlotte seems to have taken stock of her music, for there are forty-eight volumes (some containing ten or a dozen pieces) in the library in which is written in a bold hand: 'This volume belongs to the Queen. 1788.' The manuscripts include, besides the J. C. Bach autographs,[2] music by Araja, J. S. Bach and Graun; in the engraved music, consisting of keyboard and chamber works, English publications predominate, but there are also some good French editions and a remarkable volume of German harpsichord pieces, all published by J. U. Haffner of Nuremberg *c.* 1750–55. These are now unique in British libraries and exceedingly rare elsewhere. It would be most interesting to know who advised the Queen in her choice of music, whether in Germany or England, and whether it was the same person who inscribed her volumes in such a bold hand.[3] Its style strongly resembles and is probably identical with that in which many notes of imperfections are written on leaves inserted in the Handel autographs. Chrysander[4] suggested a date (of *c.* 1780) for these notes, but was unaware of this similarity.

[1] See W. T. Parke, *Musical Memoirs* (London, 1830), vol. I, p. 226.

[2] The music in the Fitzwilliam Museum includes three more volumes of manuscripts in J. C. Bach's autograph, with the same inscription and date and presented by C. Fairfax Murray in 1917. The binding, half red morocco with marbled paper sides, is identical with many volumes in the Royal Music Library.

[3] That this is not the writing of Queen Charlotte herself is shown by comparison with a volume of her autograph letters, dating from this period, B.M. Add. MS. 33131. [This problem is, of course, solved in the second article of this Appendix.]

[4] Note between p. 2 and p. 3 of his facsimile of the autograph of *Messiah*, 1892. The Handel autographs provided the primary source for Chrysander's Händel-Gesellschaft edition. Some account of the remarkable way in which he used them is given in my article 'Chrysander and the Royal Music Library', in *The Monthly Musical Record*, vol. LXXXIX (1959), pp. 13–24.

In addition to works which George III and Queen Charlotte either received gradually by presentation or acquired singly by purchase, it appears that the King, early in his reign, had laid the foundations of their library by buying a collection of manuscripts. The facts are these. The preface to vol. II of the catalogue states that 'The Miscellaneous Manuscripts comprising rather more than a thousand volumes, were purchased by King George III in 1762 to form the nucleus of a Royal collection'. It would be of great interest to know the source of this collection and what exactly it comprised, but the authority for the statement cannot now be found.[1] As the sum paid must have been substantial, it might be expected that some record of it would exist; but there is no trace of the purchase in the Royal Archives at Windsor for 1762, nor in sources at the Public Record Office.

Such a total lack of information is the more regrettable as the numerical exactitude of the statement is open to question. The total of miscellaneous manuscript compositions now in the royal collection and indisputably written before 1762 does not exceed 750, and the number of volumes (in many of which a dozen or more pieces are bound together) is considerably fewer. This total can be further reduced by a number of pre-1762 manuscripts acquired at least twenty years after that date. There is, however, a residue of about 400 pieces, including some English works of the early eighteenth century, but consisting mainly of songs from Italian operas. A good many of these were written for the Teatro Argentino in Rome. While it is possible that Joseph Smith, British Consul at Venice, was the agent for part of this purchase, the complete lack of any books of musical interest in his library which was sold to George III does not lend colour to this idea. The few notes of previous ownership in the manuscripts are unhelpful. At present, then, this royal purchase remains a curiosity as much of arithmetic as of provenance. May not its exaggerated total have come from round figures given by some letter-writer or diarist of the time?

---

[1] It is to be presumed that Squire had this knowledge, but very few of his papers or notes, other than letters, now survive.

Another group of books added later in the eighteenth century was a very fine collection of madrigals, 'most of which were formerly in the possession of Sir John Hawkins'.[1] This statement presumably refers to the collection of English, French, Italian and Dutch part-books, now in a uniform binding of not earlier than *c.* 1770 and not later than *c.* 1805. As Hawkins's whole library was burnt in 1785,[2] the addition must be earlier than that date. Some other interesting printed and manuscript items came from the sale of William Boyce's very fine library which was auctioned at Christie's on 14 April 1779. Two of the most important volumes were the twelve autograph *sinfonie* of Alessandro Scarlatti and the Cosyn Virginal Book. The provenance of both has been unknown hitherto and even now the channel through which they came into royal ownership remains obscure.[3] Another great treasure added during this period is the volume of autographs by Henry Purcell, presented by Dr Philip Hayes 'at an unknown date'.[4]

By the late seventeen-seventies the Prince of Wales began collecting music, and before he became Prince Regent had amassed a notable collection of printed instrumental and chamber music, now mostly identifiable by his crest on the covers. This was doubtless used for the concerts he gave at Carlton House—possibly also for those at the Brighton Pavilion—but exactly where it was kept is uncertain. One volume[5] bears a pencil note 'From the King's Room for the Music Room. May 1820. G. Troup'.[6] This at least suggests that there a collection of some kind was kept together. Further evidence of the Prince of Wales's wide interest in music is perhaps

---

[1] Barclay Squire, in *Grove*, s.v. 'Musical Libraries', 1st ed. 1890, vol. II, p. 423; 2nd ed. 1900, vol. II, p. 707: this statement was modified in the 3rd edition to 'Italian madrigals'.

[2] P. A. Scholes, *Life & Activities of Sir John Hawkins* (London, 1953), p. 157.

[3] [The obscurity alluded to in this paragraph is, like the problem mentioned in note 3, p. 108 above, cleared up in the second article of this Appendix.]

[4] So stated in an unsigned article 'The King's Music' in *The Times*, 13 February 1911. (The article was in fact by Squire: there is a copy of it in vol. III of his bound miscellanea, now in the library of Pembroke College, Cambridge.) The date of the royal binding on this volume lies between *c.* 1770 and *c.* 1780. Cf. note 4, p. 128 below.

[5] Alexander Campbell, *Albyn's Anthology* (Edinburgh, 1816).

[6] George Troup was Wardrobe Keeper in the Household of the Prince of Wales. See *The Royal Kalendar...for the Year 1820* (London [1819?]), p. 126.

to be found in a volume which includes a motet by Palestrina and an anonymous piece of the early eighteenth century, 'Tonat coelum'. Both these bear an inscription 'To His Royal Highness the Prince of Wales. From Dr Pepusch's Library'.

There is some indication that not all the music collected by royalty in the eighteenth century remained in their collections. Besides the volumes mentioned in notes 1 and 2, pp. 107 and 108 above, there is a larger collection mentioned in *Grove*[1] as the property of Fairfax Murray: it included 'a quantity of manuscript music, formerly belonging to the Duchess of Gloucester, including much that had been in the possession of the Royal Family of George III'. This cannot at present be traced. Even before the Georgian era drew to its close, a new generation of royal music-lovers had begun to collect, though mostly on a small scale. The Duchess of Kent owned a copy (lacking the first volume) of *The Harmonicon* (1824–33), an enterprising journal with a European outlook which gave, *inter alia*, accounts of new, difficult works by Beethoven. In 1830 Thomas Moore wrote a respectful dedication on one of his songs and sent it to the Duchess. She herself composed some charming songs, one of which she dedicated to her daughter, Queen Victoria, on her wedding day, 10 February 1840. This, and other songs (not, apparently, in autograph) are written on music paper with an elegant decorated border, an early example of printing by chromo-lithography.

Both as Princess and Queen, Victoria collected a good deal of music. It can be identified sometimes by her signature, sometimes by the initials 'V.R.' on the spine or 'The Queen' on the upper cover of the binding, which is dull compared both with the noble style chosen by her Hanoverian ancestors and the many splendidly bound volumes presented during her reign. Her personal music reflected her love of playing the piano, both solo and in duets, principally Schubert and Beethoven; her vocal music included works by Mercadente, Bellini, Donizetti, Schubert and, later, Pacini and Gounod.

[1] 2nd ed. 1906, vol. II, p. 708. See also note 2, p. 108 above.

The Queen's pianoforte teacher, both before and after her accession, was Mrs Lucy Anderson,[1] who later also taught the Princesses. Her husband, George Frederick Anderson,[2] was a violinist of some distinction, who succeeded Franz Cramer in 1848 as Master of the Queen's Musick, and held the post till 1870. As volumes bearing the names of both the Andersons are found in the Royal Music Library, it seems likely that they took an interest in the collection. There are, inscribed to Mrs Anderson by the several composers, the full and vocal scores of Sterndale Bennett's *May Queen*, a song by Bishop, as well as a programme of one of Ella's Musical Union Concerts. From her, too, must surely have come a good copy of Playford's *Choice Ayres* (Books 1–5, 1676–84) inscribed 'John Philpot 1802'. George Anderson added inscribed copies of two operas in full score by George Onslow, a vocal score of Mozart's *Nozze di Figaro*, and a volume of rare violin duets. Thus, as in the eighteenth century, the collection grew through the interest of those in royal service.

During the mid nineteenth century, and even beyond it, the genius of the Music Library was the Prince Consort.[3] His influence was twofold—first, through the many pieces which his active patronage brought into it, both from English composers and from his gifted kinsfolk in his own and a later generation; second, through the bequest of music from his own library at his death in 1861.[4] The Prince was himself a composer, of small choral works and songs, some of which bear his autograph dedication to Queen Victoria. His brothers, Ernst, Duke of Saxe-Coburg and Gotha, and Ernst, Duke of Saxe-Meiningen, are represented by large-scale operas. King Georg V of Hanover enjoyed the musical dignity of a *Gesamtausgabe* of his songs and

---

[1] 1797–1878, daughter of John Philpot, a music-master of Bath, appointed pianist to Queen Adelaide in 1831. She is described in J. D. Brown's *Biographical Dictionary of Musicians* (Paisley, 1886), as 'in her day, the best pianist in England'. She achieved the distinction of having been the first lady pianist to play at a Philharmonic Society concert, on 24 April 1822, when she performed Hummel's B minor concerto. A short account of her, with a charming portrait, is in *The London Spring Annual*...(1833), pp. 16, 17. She married G. F. Anderson in 1820.

[2] 1793–1876. Brown (*op. cit.*) says he was a man of great influence: he was Treasurer of the Philharmonic Society and of the Royal Society of Musicians.

[3] There is a fascinating account of the Prince's musical tastes and activities in Sir Theodore Martin's *Life of His Royal Highness the Prince Consort* (London, 1875), vol. I, Appendix A (pp. 485–510).

[4] According to the preface to vol. II of the catalogue.

piano pieces: in the eighteen-nineties Ernst, Grand Duke of Hesse-Darm-stadt and the Emperor Wilhelm II, both published songs and presented copies, affectionately inscribed, to Queen Victoria. The collection includes other works by members of the German royal houses.

It was presumably the Prince Consort who induced Queen Victoria to subscribe to the great editions published by the Bach-Gesellschaft and the Händel-Gesellschaft.[1] From 1840 to 1848 the Prince Consort directed the Concerts of Ancient Music whose library[2] was kept at Buckingham Palace. His own music and musical literature, of which forty-nine pieces can be identified from the elegant black stamp 'The Prince Consort's Library', reflect a range of musical interests visible in the programmes of the Ancient Concerts, which include music from 1520 onwards. His taste in music was as remarkable as was his taste in the visual arts. It is probable that many of his music-books, besides those bearing his stamp, are now in the Royal Music Library. Though Queen Victoria may not have shared the Prince Consort's more recondite musical tastes, they were united in their enthu-siasm for Mendelssohn, who when in London was a regular visitor to the Palace, and presented signed and sealed copies of his music to *Oedipus at Colonus* and *Athalia*. The performance of *Oedipus* given at Buckingham Palace on 10 February 1848 was the first in England.

In 1870 G. F. Anderson was succeeded as Master of the Queen's Musick by W. G. Cusins (1833–93, knighted 1892) a composer and conductor of note in his day, who discharged his royal office greatly to the benefit of the Library. He added some interesting manuscripts of early-nineteenth-century Italian operas, and the 1682 score of Lully's *Persée* which he purchased at Puttick's in 1875. In November 1879 Grove wrote[3] to Julian Marshall that Cusins was actively interested in the Library. His various pencil annotations in the Handel autographs show that he examined them closely and intel-ligently. His notable pamphlet on *Messiah* sources appeared in 1874. He

---

[1] Later she subscribed to the complete editions of Schubert, Palestrina and Purcell, but not, rather curiously, to that of Beethoven which began in 1866.

[2] After the Concerts ceased in 1848, Queen Victoria presented it to the Royal College of Music.

[3] Unpublished letter in a volume of Handel catalogues, etc., written by Marshall (R.M. 18.b.2).

also confirmed Gounod's somewhat improbable ownership of the rare *Geist- und Lehr-reicher Kirchen und Hauss-Buch* of 1694 (with the fine frontis-piece of Schütz among his singers) and possibly secured it for the collection. Not the least of Cusins's services was to begin a full-length catalogue of which, unfortunately, only the section for sacred music was printed, without title-page or date.[1] Probably his death in 1893 cut it short.

During Cusins's term of office there fell the Jubilee of 1887 which brought many additions to the Library in the form of loyal musical tributes. In 1897, under his successor Sir Walter Parratt, these were even more numer-ous. Not the least remarkable was a volume of twelve songs composed by Queen Liliuokalani of Hawaii (printed by the Pacific Music Company in San Francisco) and sent to Queen Victoria with a verbose and somewhat fulsome letter from the composer on the back of which is written 'not noticed'. In July 1899 Leoncavallo inscribed to the Queen vocal scores of his operas *La Bohème* and *Chatterton*. These, like the first issue of Verdi's *Aïda*, and many other nineteenth-century items, are virtually mint, in the original printed covers. One of the last pieces which the Queen received from an eminent English musician was *The Absent-Minded Beggar*, set by Sullivan to Kipling's famous words, with an autograph dedication from the composer dated November 1899.

Among Queen Victoria's children, only King Edward VII, with Queen Alexandra, contributed much to the Library. Of the small quantity of his music, fourteen volumes contain his bookplates both as Prince of Wales and Sovereign, the latter plate with the word 'Sandringham' prominent. The most unusual item among them is a scarce collection of bagpipe music pub-lished in 1869 by William Ross, who was pipe-major to Queen Victoria. Queen Alexandra's name appears on the binding of a score of volumes (which sometimes include her charming bookplate) of miscellaneous piano music, mostly by Beethoven and his contemporaries. More interesting are her vocal scores of Offenbach's *La Périchole*, *Barbe-Bleu* and *Princesse de*

[1] Barclay Squire, s.v. 'Musical Libraries' in the 1st edition of *Grove* (1890), vol. II, p. 422, wrote that this catalogue would supersede the manuscript catalogue made at the beginning of the nineteenth century. No trace of this manuscript can now be found either at Windsor Castle or Buckingham Palace.

*Trébizonde*, all acquired during a visit to Paris in 1868. King Edward's ownership of Lecocq's *Fille de Madame Angot* points to a sympathetic interest in French operetta.

Such, in outline, are the provenance and association of some of the volumes in this great library. Their interest in this regard would be much enhanced by some knowledge of their arrangement on the shelves of their past owners. But here there is a 'universal blank'. Not a single early shelf-mark is to be found, nor were any given later when the library was unified, probably by Cusins, towards the end of the nineteenth century. The old manuscript catalogue, which cannot now be found, would probably have contained a good deal of evidence. Even the evidence of bindings is mostly inconclusive, because although several groups of books are bound in similar styles, it seems pretty certain from internal dates and from the continued use of certain forms of lettering and ornaments that a style might persist for two or three decades. When Barclay Squire first saw the collection at Buckingham Palace in *c.* 1905 or earlier, it seems to have been kept in the room of the 'Master of the Music' which was regarded as unsafe, for later he wrote: 'The collection has recently been moved into a fire-proof room in the basement of the Palace.'[1] In February 1911, before the transfer of the books to the British Museum in March, Squire, with a colleague named F. W. Jekyll, went to the Palace, and made a shelf-list in manuscript (now R.M. 19.f.17) but the entries in it are so brief, and the subsequent rearrangement of the books so drastic, that practically nothing can be gleaned from it.

## 2. FREDERICK NICOLAY IN THE SERVICE OF QUEEN CHARLOTTE

On p. 108 of the preceding article I alluded briefly to two categories of manuscript annotations which were written in two groups of music-books, namely, the collection which belonged to Queen Charlotte, and the Handel

---

[1] *Grove* (2nd ed. 1906), vol. II, p. 707. In a later, retrospective memorandum submitted to the Trustees of the British Museum in 1920, Squire describes this room as 'fire-proof (but not damp-proof)'.

manuscripts, both autographs and copies. Every volume of the Queen's bears, usually on the front endpaper, the words 'This volume belongs to the Queen. 1788' (Pl. VI), followed by a list of contents if it contains several publications bound together. This note occurs in forty-eight volumes. Among the Handel manuscripts, thirty-three volumes of autographs and five of copies bear, on the front endpaper or on bound-in slips or full-page blanks, a total of fifty-three annotations which give information about contents, imperfections (Pl. V), misbound numbers and the like. In my previous article, I hazarded the identity of the handwriting of these two sets of notes, but felt I could not make a positive assertion. Subsequently, however, a systematic comparison of all the contents-lists of Queen Charlotte's books with all the Handel annotations established the fact that all are in the same hand.

But this afforded no clue to the writer. All that could be deduced from his annotations was that he must have been a person of some authority in the service of Queen Charlotte, and had studied the music of Handel's operas and oratorios. As the Handel manuscripts became George III's property between 1772 and 1774,[1] the annotations must presumably have been made with his approval and were probably written shortly before the volumes were bound in one of two styles which were in use between about 1780 and, at the latest, 1810. Thus it seemed fair to infer that the annotator would have been known also to the King, although such an inference did nothing to light a path through the forest of conjectural identifications.

The two vital hints which ultimately led to the discovery of his name both came from books in the Royal Music Library. Scrutiny of all fly-leaves for notes of ownership had revealed a copy of Byrd's *Gradualia*[2] scored in an early seventeenth-century hand, and bearing these words, written by Sir John Hawkins: 'This score I bought at Dr. Boyce's sale 16th April 1779 for 14s.'[3] This seemed worth following up, not primarily for any possible

---

[1] See p. 107.

[2] R.M. 24.c.13.

[3] In point of fact, Hawkins did not himself bid for this lot, 240. The sum of 14s. was paid by Thomas Bever. Hawkins did purchase lot 71, an ode by Maurice Greene, for £1. 14s. 6d.

relevance to Queen Charlotte's annotator, but because it might lead to the identification of other volumes which had passed from Boyce's library into royal ownership.

But no published description of this collection could be found. Copies of the sale-catalogue were ultimately traced through a brief reference in the article on Boyce in *Grove* by H. Watkins Shaw, who had located one in Gerald Coke's collection and another in Leeds Public Libraries. A photostat of the latter copy showed that the auctioneer was John Christie. But neither copy bore the names of buyers or the prices paid. Messrs Christie, however, very kindly supplied this want when they informed me, in reply to my inquiry, that all their house-copies of eighteenth-century sale-catalogues were extant, and further allowed me to copy the names of those who bid at the sale of Boyce's superb library (for such it proved to be) and the prices they paid.

The purchaser of a number of lots readily identifiable with volumes now in the Royal Music Library was 'Mr Nicolay'. The names of the other successful bidders included various musical scholars of the day, several composers, and a number of dealers. To which category might 'Mr Nicolay' have belonged? This is the name, more commonly spelt 'Nicolai', of a dozen composers active in the second half of the eighteenth century, of whom one, Valentino, had many compositions published in London.[1] It seemed reasonable to assume that, as considerable musical knowledge was needed to bid at an auction, 'Mr Nicolay' was a musician acting on behalf of the royal family. In any case, there was then no evidence to connect him with the writer of the annotations. But later chance led to the finding of this very link.

During the selection of items for the British Museum's commemorative exhibition of Handel and Purcell, I had occasion to scrutinise a volume

---

[1] All these composers are probably members of the same large German family which originated in Ober-Weisbach, a small town in Thuringia. Its main branches are fully set out in the *Deutsches Geschlechterbuch*, edited by Bernard Koerner, vol. LXXXVII (1933), pp. 447–69. Here it is stated that another branch included 'various musicians and doctors' and would be treated in another volume, which, however, has never appeared, as the work, issued at Görlitz, was suspended during the war and has since been discontinued.

comprising part of Benjamin Goodison's attempted complete edition of Purcell. This[1] I knew to contain also a remarkable sequence of five editions of the prospectus issued for this edition. On the first page of the second, at the extreme left margin, I saw, written in a minute hand (possibly Goodison's) the words '—Nicolay Esq.' (So tightly are these prospectuses sewn into the binding immediately after the endpaper that the first part of the name is hidden.) This name does not occur among the subscribers printed in the first and second editions, but in the third the list includes 'Fred. Nicolay Esq. 3 sets'. In the fourth edition, it is amplified to 'Fred. Nicolay Esq. St. James's Palace. 3 copies'. The words 'St. James's Palace' opened an entirely new line of investigation, which ultimately made it possible to reconstruct the outline of Nicolay's career in royal service, and to discover something of his family history and of his tastes as a collector of books and music.

Once he was clearly seen to be a man of position and authority,[2] it seemed paramount to find his will and trace his descendants, in case a portrait or other family documents were extant. The search for the former was fortunately limited by the date on the title-page of the sale-catalogue of Nicolay's library:

A Catalogue of the very elegant Library of the late Fred. Nicolay, Esq. of St. James's Palace, consisting of a valuable collection in history, poetry, voyages and travels, British and foreign biography, translations of the classics in English, Italian and French: belles lettres: miscellanies &c: particularly rich in Italian and French literature ...which will be sold by auction, by Leigh and S. Sotheby...on Wednesday, November 29, 1809.[3]

This led to his will at Somerset House,[4] a six-page document which is proved by an attached affidavit to be in his autograph (Pl. IV). Comparison with the two groups of annotations in the Royal Music Library shows that

---

[1] R.M. 9.i.19. See A. Hyatt King, 'Benjamin Goodison's Complete Edition of Purcell', *The Monthly Musical Record*, vol. LXXXI (1951), pp. 63–9. I must confess that I did not then notice the writing on the second edition of the prospectus: even if I had, the name 'Nicolay' would then have meant nothing, being irrelevant to the article. Goodison, incidentally, secured two lots at the Boyce sale.

[2] The sequence of facts and references as given in the following pages is far from being that of the order of discovery, which was, perhaps inevitably, a rather haphazard affair. There was, at first, no logical or historical connection between the facts as they came to light.

[3] British Museum S.C.S. 66 (3).

[4] P.C.C. 394. Loveday.

it was Nicolay who wrote both of them. In the specimens illustrated, the distinctive spacing of such letters as 'p', 'g' and 'h', 'A' and 'B' is worth noting. The outlines of the words 'The Queen' are also significant. The 'R', with the tail curving back under the first up-stroke, is highly individual.[1]

Even with such an uncommon name as Nicolay, the search for descendants might have been lengthy, but for a final stroke of luck. Readers of Ralph Kirkpatrick's *Domenico Scarlatti*[2] will remember how the author, having exhausted archival sources in Madrid for material relating to the composer's life and descendants, had recourse to the city's telephone directory, and there found living descendants who possessed a considerable amount of unknown family papers. The London telephone directory yielded no Nicolays, but the provincial ones a dozen or so. Now the *Dictionary of National Biography* includes Sir William Nicolay,[3] a distinguished soldier whose career included service at Waterloo and ended with the successive governorships of Dominica, Antigua and Mauritius. The probable continuance of a family tradition suggested that anyone of this name now in the Services might be a descendant. I therefore first approached Colonel B. U. Nicolay, C.B.,[4] whose name appeared in the Surrey telephone directory. He proved to be a descendant in the fourth generation, not directly from Frederick Nicolay, but from his brother Christian Frederick, who was private physician to Queen Caroline. Colonel Nicolay possessed portraits of both the brothers, and papers relating to his family's history, in which he had long been interested. His great kindness in allowing me to use his notes and see his heirlooms contributed much to the interest of this article.

From these and other sources I was able to form the following outline of Frederick Nicolay's life. He was born in 1728 or 1729[5] in Saxe-Gotha, the

[1] Further comparison with a letter written by Nicolay about 1795 (now in the archives of the Royal Society of Musicians and kindly dated for me by F. E. Beyer, the Secretary) shows that Nicolay's hand altered little throughout the last thirty years or so of his life.

[2] Princeton, 1945, pp. 134, 135.

[3] The *D.N.B.* is vague as to his ancestry: he was actually the third son of Frederick Nicolay.

[4] d. 8 December 1960. The portrait of Frederick Nicolay was reproduced in *The Book Collector* (Winter 1960), facing p. 408.

[5] In his will, he expressed the wish to be buried in the churchyard of 'St Michael Royal'. *The Register of Baptisms and Burials of St Michael Paternoster Royal, London*, edited by Thomas C. Dale (1934), p. 334 (typescript, in the library of the Society of Genealogists), gives his age at burial as 80.

elder son of Gaspard (or Caspar) and Sapphira Nicolay. Frederick and his younger brother Christian Frederick were brought to England in 1736 by their parents when they travelled in the suite of Princess Augusta.[1] The young Frederick seems early to have shown 'the refined and courtly manners'[2] which later endeared him to the royal family, for in 1751 he was appointed 'assistant to Dancing Master' to George III as Prince of Wales, at a salary of £50.[3] His musical gifts, too, were early in evidence, for in this same year on 3 March he was admitted to membership of the Society for Decayed Musicians (now the Royal Society of Musicians), being then about twenty-three, the youngest possible age for admission.[4] The various stages in Nicolay's career at Court cannot, unfortunately, all be dated exactly, for the printed Kalendars are inexact, and the Royal Archives at Windsor Castle are not complete for this period. Undoubtedly he rose quickly in royal favour. In August 1761 he was one of those selected by George III to escort Princess Sophia Charlotte of Mecklenburg-Strelitz to England.[5] This is confirmed by two independent statements in the Nicolay Papers. On the stormy voyage from Cuxhaven, Nicolay became aware of the musical tastes of his future royal mistress. Her first biographer wrote: 'She did not appear the least affected by the tediousness of her passage: on the contrary she continued all the time in good health and spirits, and frequently played on the harpsichord, practising English tunes for the purpose of gratifying the taste of her new subjects.'[6] Nicolay was appointed a Page of the Backstairs to Queen Charlotte on 20 July 1762[7] and quickly won her esteem. In

---

[1] See B.M. Add. MS. 38361, f. 276: memorial, dated 18 November 1811, of Augusta Georgiana Nicolay to the Prince Regent: 'The grandfather of your memorialist came to England with the late Princess Dowager of Wales in the year 1736.' Confirmed by family tradition, and by Add. MS. 37836 'General List of Establishment of the Prince and Princess of Wales, Lady Day 1738 (–1751). (Most appointments made in 1736)', f. 3, Page of the Presence—Caspar Nicolay.

[2] Nicolay Papers.          [3] B.M. Add. MS. 37836, f. 7.

[4] Information from F. E. Beyer.

[5] See *The Gentleman's Magazine* (January–June 1809), p. 486.

[6] Walley Chamberlain Oulton, *Authentic and impartial Memoirs of her late Majesty, Charlotte, Queen of Great Britain and Ireland* (London, 1819), p. 17. There is a rather more vivid description in *Court and Private Life in the Time of Queen Charlotte, being the Journals of Mrs Papendiek* (London, 1887), vol. I, p. 7. Mrs Papendiek wrote that the Princess 'did not lose her gaiety through all this trying time, but sang to her harpsichord, leaving the door of her cabin open so as to encourage her companions in their misery'.

[7] P.R.O., L.C. 5. 168 (206): the *Gentleman's Magazine* gives the date of appointment as 5 September 1761.

his will he bequeathed to his eldest son, George, a 'large gold snuff box, which was a present to me from the Queen, send [*sic*] me by Mme Swellenberg on the day the Prince of Wales was born'.[1] By about 1780 Nicolay became the Queen's Principal Page, a position requiring great tact and an intimate knowledge of Court and society.

The Nicolay Papers state that one of his duties was to receive at the soirées 'all the foreigners of distinction who came over to the Court of England'—which would soon have given him a European name, not least for his musical interests and his special services in this art to the Queen. For in 1762[2] he became a member of the Queen's 'Band of Musick', and, later, of a smaller, co-existent group, entitled the 'Queen's Chamber Band'. In both of these he played the violin, which he had been taught by the famous Matthew Dubourg, a friend of Handel.[3] Since a musician of such international fame as John Christian Bach was also a member of this Band, it is not surprising that Nicolay's musical acquaintance became wide. His name appears on the visiting lists kept by Leopold Mozart and Haydn when they stayed in London respectively in 1764 and 1791.[4]

Though a member of the Queen's household, Nicolay probably owed almost equal responsibility to the King in matters musical. This is suggested by two passages found in the respective memoirs each written by the daughter of the two famous musical historians of Nicolay's day. Fanny Burney, describing the growth of her father's *Account of the Musical Performances in Westminster Abbey and the Pantheon in commemoration of Handel*, which bore a dedication to George III composed by Samuel Johnson, wrote thus:

The King himself deigned to make frequent inquiry into the state of the business: and when his Majesty knew that the publication was retarded only by the engravers, he desired to see the loose and unbound sheets of the work, which he perused with so strong an interest in their contents, that he drew up two critical notes upon them,

[1] The snuff-box was in the late Col. Nicolay's possession.     [2] *Court and City Kalendar*, pp. 93, 94.
[3] Papendiek, *Journals*, vol. 1, p. 76. The *Journals* reveal that the Nicolay and Papendiek families were long on intimate terms. Mrs Papendiek's husband Charles was flautist in the Queen's Chamber Band.
[4] Leopold Mozart, *Reiseaufzeichnungen* (Dresden, 1920), p. 33, 'Mr. Nicolai, Cammer-Page beim König, oder Reserve [?] Unter...Cammerdiener': *The Collected Correspondence and London Notebooks of Joseph Haydn*, ed. by H. C. Robbins Landon (London, 1959), p. 266, 'Nicolai, valet de chambre of the King and a composer'.

with so much perspicuity and justness, that Dr. Burney, unwilling to lose their purport, yet not daring to presume to insert them with the King's name in any appendix, cancelled the two sheets to which they had reference and embodied their meaning in his own text. At this he was certain the King could not be displeased, as it was with his Majesty's consent that they had been communicated to the doctor, by Mr. Nicolai, a page of the Queen's.[1]

Likewise, Laetitia Matilda, the daughter of Sir John Hawkins, mentions Nicolay when describing the presentation of her father's *History of Music* to George III, this too being dedicated to him:

...he [Sir John Hawkins] awaited the King's coming from the riding-house, and was conversing with Mr. Nicolay, one of the pages, who was a lover of music, when he was most agreeably surprised to see His Majesty enter the appartements, followed by the Queen. Mr. Nicolay received the presented volume from the King's hand, and then ensued a conversation on the subject of the work, and of music in general, in which Her Majesty took a lively part: the King professing his decided taste for what is called the *old school*, and jocularly complaining of his inability to persuade the Queen to prefer it to the modern style.[2]

The progressive nature of Queen Charlotte's musical taste is clearly shown by the fact that she possessed many works in the style represented by J. C. Bach, Mozart and some of his immediate forerunners, Clementi, Boccherini, and the like. These would have been mostly anathema to the King, whose enthusiasm seems to have run to Handel and little else.

Linked with other evidence, these two passages show how close Nicolay must have stood to the musical interests of both the King and the Queen, and would account for the presence of his annotations in their music-books. For the Queen's music, we have a definite contemporary statement in the entry in E. L. Gerber's *Lexicon der Tonkünstler*: 'NICOLAI (Friedrich) Kammermusikus und Violinist in der Kapelle der Königinn von England um 1783: hat auch zugleich als Bibliothekar, derselben Musik Sammlung unter den Händen.'[3]

---

[1] *Memoirs of Dr. Burney...by his daughter, Madame d'Arblay* (London, 1832), vol. II, pp. 384, 385.

[2] *Memoirs, Anecdotes, Facts, and Opinions, collected and preserved by Laetitia-Matilda Hawkins* (London, 1824), vol. II, pp. 43, 44.

[3] Leipzig, 1792, vol. II, col. 28. Though in fact Nicolay was in the Queen's Band twenty years earlier than this, the notice shows that he was known in Germany. The exact source of Gerber's information about English musicians is not made clear in his preface, but his general standard of accuracy is high.

It seems unlikely that there exists any evidence which would provide an exact date for the beginning of Nicolay's work as royal music librarian. Probably it simply grew up as part of his general duties, in the late seventeen-seventies or early seventeen-eighties. It was probably in this period that he wrote on the title-page of the manuscript catalogue of Queen Caroline's library (cf. p. 106) the following note: 'N.B. All the duplicates found in this catalogue were sent to Hanover by his Majesty's order.' Study of the Handel manuscripts suggests that he may have had something to do with the binding of them, for the blanks bearing notes in his hand must obviously have been inserted at his direction. So it is possible that the actual binding was done under his supervision, and if so he may be held responsible for one of the most appalling onslaughts ever wrought by the binder's shears on a collection of eighteenth-century musical autographs. For all three edges have been savagely cut in an attempt to reduce as many volumes as possible to a uniform size.[1] This process affected especially the autographs, where Handel's inspiration flowed freely beyond the staves on to all the margins of many pages. On some, his writing at top and bottom has actually been bled by the shears, though at the fore-edge the overflow has been respected, but left standing out on little tabs, an inch or more in height. Many of these have now become dangerously worn from repeated use.

If, however, this misguided attempt at uniformity of conservation may not be wholly to Nicolay's credit, his service in acquisition is of the highest merit. We may now turn to the Boyce sale, and the part he played in it. Nicolay was a man with such a wide acquaintance that it is not surprising to learn from the Nicolay Papers that he knew John Christie. The relevant passage runs thus: 'Frederick...was a confidential friend of the King, who employed him in all his transactions such as furnishing books, prints, etc.

---

[1] The names of the successive binders who may have been responsible are set out in an article by Charles Ramsden, 'Bookbinders to George III and his immediate Descendants and Collaterals', *The Library* (1958), pp. 186–93. Of those here listed, only John Shore and James Fraser are known to have bound music, the former for the Duke of Cumberland, the latter for George IV as Prince of Wales. Presumably they may have bound music for other members of the royal family. Queen Charlotte's binder was Charles Meyer.

He set up Christy [*sic*] the auctioneer by employing him to get things for the Court.' Christie must therefore have been gratified when Nicolay bid on 16 April 1779 at the Boyce sale. The following is the list of items against which Nicolay's name appears in the marked catalogue, with the prices paid, and identification with an item in the present Royal Music Library, whereever possible:

| Lot no. | Description | Price paid £ s. d. | Pressmark in Royal Music Library and Catalogue Reference, if required |
|---|---|---|---|
| 20 | Alessandro Scarlatti's opera, in score of Tigrane. MS | 5 6 | 23.b.28 |
| 21 | Serenata a 5 voci con instrumenti—The Four Seasons, in two Books. MS | 8 0 | Cannot now be traced |
| 27 | Scarlatti's twelve Concertos in Score, MS, the Author's Original | 4 11 0 | 21.b.14 |
| 28 | Italian Madrigals, Songs, Serenata, Cantatas, Duetos, &c by Bigongiari, Abbate Steffani, Nic. L'Haym, Alessandro Stradella. MS | 13 6 | 23.f.10 (vol. II, pp. 26, 83, 195, 201, 207) |
| 33 | Sinfonia by Scarlatti, and Palestrina—Mottets—Ditto by Carissimi, Gratiani, Fabri, Checcheli, and Florido Basso. MS | 1 0 0 | 24.c.10 (vol. II, pp. 40, 41, 62, 79, 150). (The *Sinfonia* by Scarlatti is not in 24.c.10: this may be 24.I.13 (I), separated when the Boyce volume was rebound) |
| 34 | Cantatas, Duettos by Nic. L'Haym, Bononcini, Steffani, Giovanni del Violone, A. Scarlatti and Carissimi. MS | 11 0 | 23.f.4 (vol. II, pp. 258, 259) |
| 46 | Constantino, an opera, second and third acts, one part wanting. MS | | *Constantino* cannot now be traced |
| 47 | Duetti a camera, P. Torri, Steffani, and Handel MS | 11 0 | 23.f.9 (vol. II, pp. 83, 195, 201, 203, 213) |
| 67 | Phaeton, an opera, by Lully, an elegant Score. MS | 5 0 | 21.h.11 (vol. II, p. 119) |

| Lot no. | Description | Price paid £ s. d. | Pressmark in Royal Music Library and Catalogue Reference, if required |
|---|---|---|---|
| 68 | Proserpine, le Triomphe de l'amour, two Operas, by Lully | 5 0 | 12.a.b, 12.a.10 |
| 69 | Du Temple de la Paix, by Lully—Lambert's Airs, for two, three and four Voices | 5 0 | 21.a.8 (1) and 13.f.8 (vol. III, pp. 201, 189, assuming both these to be printed, not MS). |
| 166 | Magnificat, with instruments, Roma. MS.—Laudate Dominum omnes gentes, MS. Del Sig. J. Georgi, with Parts. Dixit Dominus. MS. Colona—Confitebor. MS. Buceto.—Laudate pueri, with parts MS.—Missa in canone, del Sig. Fux. MS | 2 8 0 | 24.a.10 (vol. II, pp. 45, 64, 70, 239) |
| 199 | Duettos by Abbate Steffani, MS.—Ditto by Marcello, MS. a celebrated Venetian nobleman, a very fine Collection | 2 5 0 | 23.k.21 (vol. II, pp. 205, 206) |
| 212 | La Mascarade.—La Feste de l'amour e de Bacchus, by Lully.—Alceste, ditto, elegantly written | 9 0 | 21.h.13 (1, 2) (vol. II, p. 119). 21.h.15 (vol. II, p. 118) |
| 213 | Cadmus, Psiche, MS. by Lully | 5 0 | 21.h.14, 21.h.12 (vol. II, pp. 118, 119). 12.a.1 (vol. III, p. 202, assuming this to be a printed score) |
| 215 | Achille et Polyxene, à Paris, 1686. Les Indes Galantes, par Mons. Rameau | 7 6 | 10.a.11 (vol. III, p. 273—possibly, if printed) |
| 223 | A very venerable book of Lessons, for the Organ, &c. by some of the most eminent composers in Queen Elizabeth's and King James's Reign, with many Services, in score. MS. extremely curious | 1 2 0 | 23.l.4 (vol. II, p. 48. The Cosyn Virginal Book) |

| Lot no. | Description | Price paid £ s. d. | Pressmark in Royal Music Library and Catalogue Reference, if required |
|---|---|---|---|
| 228 | A fine Score of Duettos, MS by Abbate Steffani | 2  11  0 | Probably 23.1.1–3 (vol. II, pp. 199, 200) or 23.k.7–8. The price suggests a lot in more than 1 vol. |
| 248 | A very fine Score of Ludovic de Victoria's Mottets, in one Vol. MS.—A curious copy of Pergolesi's Stabat Mater, MS. in Score | 1  11  6 | 24.a.7 (vol. II, pp. 217, 218). 24.b.8, or 22.m.5 (vol. II, p. 159) |
|  |  | £19  14  0 |  |

What gives these royal purchases such unusual interest is their generally 'antiquarian' nature, for they consist mainly of music which by 1779 was either out of fashion, or rapidly becoming so. Consequently it seems almost certain that the books must have been bought for George III, to increase the representation of the 'old school' in his collection, and not for Queen Charlotte. Apart from the fact that they do not bear Nicolay's note of her ownership, such volumes would have been quite at variance with her interest in the modern music of her day. But the King's own knowledge of music was too limited for him to venture unadvised into the antiquarian field. Frederick Nicolay, from his own musical knowledge, could hardly have advised on the preliminary choice, though as a collector himself he was perfectly competent to bid, and must have been happy at the additions to the royal collection. The adviser must surely have been either Burney or Hawkins, for both men were known personally to the King.

The evidence is scanty, and indirect, but it seems to point to Hawkins. We have some testimony that he presented a collection of madrigals to the royal library.[1] We know that he acquired from the Boyce sale a manuscript of Byrd's *Gradualia*, and presumably presented this also.[2] If we accept the

[1] See p. 33.    [2] See p. 116.

account, written by his daughter, of his meeting with the King and Queen, he certainly knew of the former's antiquarian interest. There is also Hawkins's known admiration for Steffani (whose name occurs in four lots), and his appreciation of the lesser kind of Italian composers well represented in this purchase. Burney, though a collector with a great music library, did not bid in person at the Boyce sale, nor is he known to have presented any music direct to the royal library or to have shown any interest in its growth.

In the light of Nicolay's connection with royal books, his own library deserves some mention. Its scope is fairly reflected in the title of the sale-catalogue quoted above, and it reflects the interests of a catholic and highly cultivated mind. There were 1852 lots in the sale, comprising some 3500 volumes: they fetched £1101. 16s. 6d. Rather curiously, there was only a score of lots consisting of music or books on music, mostly the latter. Apart from Morley's *Plaine and easie Introduction* (1597) and Zarlino's *Tutte l'opere* (3 vols. 1589), all the music-books were of the eighteenth century. We know from the subscription lists found occasionally in music of the same period that Nicolay possessed some other music which was excluded from the sale. He subscribed to the following: Antonio Besozzi, *Six Solos for the Flute* (1759); Samuel Arnold, *Cathedral Music* (1790); William Hayes, *Cathedral Music* (1795); William Boyce, *Anthems* (1780); Handel, full scores of *Judas Maccabaeus* (Randall, 1769) and of *Solomon* and *Susanna* (Wright, 1785?; 1784); Elizabeth Hardin, *Six Lessons for the Harpsichord* (c. 1770); Jane Guest, *Six Sonatas*, op. 1. None of these is in the auction-catalogue.

Such music as this suggests a rather conservative taste. Perhaps these missing items were included in clauses in his will where he bequeathed to his second son Frederick 'that part of my music, printed and manuscript that comes under the denomination of vocal (excepting the Three and Twenty volumes of Handel's Oratorios) also that part of my music, instrumental, where the Harpsichord part is the principal', and to his third son, William 'my best violin, made by Gernerius [*sic*], and my Tenor, made by Forster ...also that part of my music denominated instrumental'. The twenty-three volumes of Handel were not bequeathed elsewhere in his will and cannot now be traced. They might have had some interest in relation to Nicolay's annotations in the Handel manuscripts. Nicolay also owned various manuscript music, two volumes of which have found their way into the Department of Manuscripts in the British Museum. One is a score of G. B. Peschetti's opera *Il Vello d'oro*[1] with Nicolay's signature on the title-page. The other, Hasse's *Ciro conosciuto*,[2] contains his bookplate—two winged cherubs, one kneeling, one standing, holding between them an open volume inscribed 'Frederici Nicolai et amicorum'. Another manuscript of a different kind of interest is the copy which he made of the full score of *Orione* composed by his friend J. C. Bach. This, now at Tenbury (MS. 348), bears a note in Nicolay's hand to the effect that the autograph 'was destroyed by fire in the Opera House'.

Books and music must have been a great consolation in his last years, saddened as they were in the royal household by the declining health of the King. It is surely not fanciful to see a reflection of this sadness in the gradual shrinking of the Queen's Chamber Band, which dwindled in the Royal Kalendar from five members in 1782 to two in 1809, Frederick Nicolay and C. Papendiek. Nicolay died on 16 May 1809[3] after nearly sixty years in royal service, having risen to a position of high trust and authority.

So far as is known, he is the first of such standing in the royal household who also included the care of music among his duties. Although (*pace* Gerber) he had no official status as royal music librarian, some of his work was undoubtedly in the nature of librarianship. Besides what has been described in this essay, he probably did much else that is unknown at present to build up the royal collection and care for it.[4] Nicolay's portrait and hand-

---

[1] Egerton MS. 2488.   [2] Add. MS. 32026.

[3] The notice of Nicolay's death appeared in the *Gentleman's Magazine* (January–June 1809), p. 486. His successor, William Duncan, was appointed by warrant dated 7 June 1809 (P.R.O., L.S. 13. 204 (157)), the appointment being back-dated to the day of Nicolay's death.

[4] He may, for instance, have contributed to, and perhaps even have been the compiler of, a catalogue of the royal music still available at Buckingham Palace in 1904. Though it cannot now be traced, this catalogue is mentioned by H. E. Wooldridge and G. E. P. Arkwright, *Purcell's Dramatic Music*, vol. II, p. 1 (Purcell Society Edition, 1904). They state that the catalogue was written after 1768 and record that the great volume mainly in Purcell's autograph had come as a gift to the King from Dr Philip Hayes. This suggests that the catalogue might have given the sources of other acquisitions, with which Nicolay would then surely have been concerned.

writing combine with other evidence to suggest that he was a man of foresight, strong character and deliberate mind. Let the last word come from his friend Mrs Papendiek, who described him as 'a clever and excellent man'.[1] Though her opinions have sometimes been criticised as partial, here, at least, those who now use the older books in the Royal Music Library will endorse her judgement with gratitude.

[1] *Journals*, vol. I, p. 16.

# APPENDIX B

# CLASSIFIED LISTS OF PAST COLLECTORS

## ARRANGEMENT

The lists are grouped as follows:

(1) Collectors whose music was sold by auction:
  (*a*) Named collectors.
  (*b*) Unnamed collectors.
(2) Collectors whose music has been conserved intact, in whole or part, by gift or bequest, by private purchase, by inheritance, or by deposit on loan in an institutional library.
(3) Collectors whose music has been dispersed, by a bequest of which no trace can be found, by sale (either in sections by private treaty, or as separate items in a dealer's catalogue), or in other circumstances, known or unknown.
(4) Collectors for whose exact status the historical evidence is at present insufficient.

Where disposal of the music falls into two or more of groups (1), (2) and (3), the name of the owner is repeated in each as required.

The order in each group is chronological.

## GROUP 1

## COLLECTORS WHOSE MUSIC WAS SOLD BY AUCTION

### INTRODUCTORY NOTE

For sales which took place up to the end of the year 1900, the location of the sale-catalogue shown in the fourth column is that of the copy in the British Museum (with few exceptions, which may be explained in a note), as given in its *List of Catalogues of English Book Sales, 1676–1900* (London, 1915).

For sales which took place from 1900 onwards, no location of a sale-catalogue is given. Copies of most of them can be found in the British Museum by giving the pressmark S.C., with the name of the firm and the date of the sale.

The British Museum has a complete file of the catalogues issued by Messrs Puttick & Simpson and by Messrs Sotheby & Co. since their inception. All these bear the names of the buyers and the prices paid. For two other firms—Lewis, and Wheatley—who occasionally held sales of music, the Museum has a file of priced catalogues. But those issued by the few other firms found in Group I are unpriced, with the exception of the collection of catalogues made by Sir George Smart (pressmark C.61.h.1), many of which bear names and prices in his hand.

The following abbreviations for all forms of the successive partnership of well-known firms of auctioneers have been used in the third column:

Christie: Christie, Manson & Woods.
Hodgson: Hodgson & Co.
Puttick: Puttick & Simpson.
Sotheby: Sotheby & Co.

For firms which flourished in the eighteenth and nineteenth centuries but which are now defunct, only the surname is given.

For certain sales, no copy of a catalogue is known. Reference is given in the fourth column either to the source for the fact that a sale took place, or, if this cannot be stated briefly, to the relevant page in the text of the book. For a few early sales, only the place is known, and this is given in a note.

### (a) NAMED COLLECTORS

| Date of sale | Name | Auctioneer, etc. | Location of sale-catalogue, or source of information |
|---|---|---|---|
| **1711** | | | |
| 20 Dec. | Robert Orme | —[1] | *Spectator*, 27 Nov.; *Daily Courant*, 7, 19 Dec. |
| **1714** | | | |
| 6–8 Dec. | Thomas Britton | —[2] | Hawkins (1853), pp. 792, 793 |

[1] 'at the new House next the Wheat-Sheaf, in Henrietta Street.' Quoted by Michael Tilmouth, *A Calendar of References to Music in Newspapers published in London and the Provinces (1660–1719)*, R.M.A. Research Chronicle, no. 1 (1961), p. 80.

[2] 'at Mr. Ward's House in Red Bull-Yard in Clerkenwell.'

| Date of sale | Name | Auctioneer, etc. | Location of sale-catalogue, or source of information |
|---|---|---|---|
| *c.* **1750** | | | |
| n.d. | William Corbett | —[1] | Hawkins (1853), p. 823 |
| **1752** | | | |
| n.d. | Johann Christoph Pepusch | — | Hawkins (1853), pp. 907, 908 |
| **1763** | | | |
| 26 March | Ephraim Kelner | Paterson (Essex St) | Hawkins (1853), p. 908 |
| **1764** | | | |
| 23 July | William Young | Prestage (Standlinch, nr Salisbury) | 824.b.17 (11) |
| **1766** | | | |
| July | John Travers | — | Hawkins (1853), p. 908 |
| **1777** | | | |
| 26, 27 May | William Gostling | Langford | Hirsch IV, 1083 |
| **1778** | | | |
| 14 April | William Boyce, the elder | Christie | Leeds Public Library; Coke Collection |
| **1786** | | | |
| 24 June | John Stanley | Christie | 7805.e.5 (25) |
| **1795** | | | |
| 18, 19 May | Paul Stobler | — | Warren[2] |
| **1797** | | | |
| 16 May | Edmund Thomas Warren, afterwards Warren-Horne (first sale) | Sotheby | S.C.S. 30 (6) |
| *c.* **1798** | | | |
| n.d. | William and Philip Hayes | —[3] | C. 61.h.1 (12) |
| **1798** | | | |
| 7, 8 June | Thomas Bever | White | *Gentleman's Magazine*, vol. LXVIII, p. 517 |
| **1799** | | | |
| 25 June | Samuel Howard | White | Hirsch IV. 1083.a |
| **1802** | | | |
| 9 March | [Mr Balham] (lots 384–90 only consist of music) | Sotheby | S.C.S. 39 (14) |
| **1807** | | | |
| 8 June | Mr Guise (?Richard Guise)[4] | — | Warren[2] |
| **1808** | | | |
| n.d. | John Walkden | — | pp. 16, 17 |

[1] 'at his house in Silver St. near Pulteney St.'

[2] 'Warren' denotes a sale-catalogue once in the collection of Joseph Warren, and listed by him in the autograph catalogue of his music library: see pp. 92, 93.

[3] A sale-catalogue with printed prices, published at Smart's Music Warehouse.

[4] See Hughes-Hughes, vol. II, p. 937.

# Classified Lists of Past Collectors

| Date of sale | Name | Auctioneer, etc. | Location of sale-catalogue, or source of information |
|---|---|---|---|
| **1809** | | | |
| 6 Feb. | William Kitchiner (first sale) | Sotheby | S.C.S. 63 (4) |
| 9 Feb. | François Hippolyte Barthélemon | — | Warren[1] |
| **1810** | | | |
| 8 Jan. | Edmund Thomas Warren, afterwards Warren-Horne (second sale) <br> J. C. Davis | Sotheby | S.C.S. 66 (5) |
| 21 June | Daniel Walker | — | Warren[1] |
| 26 Dec. | Venanzio Rauzzini | Mrs Plura (Bath) | p. 91 |
| **1811** | | | |
| 6 March | Venanzio Rauzzini (?second sale) | (Bath) | p. 91 |
| 8 May | Henry Compton | Sotheby | S.C.S. 72 (4) |
| **1813** | | | |
| 16, 17 Feb. | Rev. John Parker | White | S.C. 1076 (5) |
| 18 May | Robert Smith | White | Hirsch IV, 1091 |
| 8 Nov. | John Sydney | Sotheby | S.C.S. 83 (4) |
| n.d. | — Ashley | — | p. 92 |
| **1814** | | | |
| 7 Feb. | Granville Sharp | Sotheby | S.C.S. 84 (7) |
| 18 May | Samuel Harrison <br> John Baptist Malchair | White | S.C. 1076 (2) |
| 8–16 Aug. | Charles Burney | White | C. 61.h.1 (12) |
| **1816** | | | |
| 21 May | John Baptist Cramer | White | C. 61.h.1 (13) |
| 24 June | J. C. Flack | — | Warren[1] |
| 2 July | Henry Harington (lots 1–95 only, in a mixed sale) | Sotheby | S.C.S. 96 (4) |
| 4 July | Samuel Webbe | White | C. 61.h.1 (14) |
| **1818** | | | |
| 23 Feb. | John Carter (lots 179–234 only are of music) | Sotheby | S.C.S. 105 (3) |
| **1819** | | | |
| 15 April | John Wall Callcott | White | Cambridge University Library, L. 27.58 (4) |
| **1820** | | | |
| 8 June | George Ebenezer Williams | White | 7897.d.13 (1) |
| **1821** | | | |
| 14 Feb. | Giuseppe Naldi | Oxenham | 7897.d.13 (2) |

[1] See p. 132, n. 2.

| Date of sale | Name | Auctioneer, etc. | Location of sale-catalogue, or source of information |
|---|---|---|---|
| **1822** | | | |
| 20–7 Feb. | John Bartleman | White | C. 61.h.1 (16) |
| 20 Nov. | Henry Hinckley | Musgrave | S.C. 1078 (4) |
| **1823** | | | |
| 12, 13 Feb. | William Dowding | Musgrave | S.C. 1078 (5) |
| 10 Dec. | Rev. Dr Monkhouse | Musgrave | 7897.d.13 (5) |
| **1824** | | | |
| 9 Feb. | Edward Jones, Bard to the King (first sale) | Sotheby | S.C.S. 134 (6) |
| 29 March | William Boyce, the younger | Musgrave | S.C. 1078 (6) |
| 1 June | John Gunn | Musgrave | 7897.d.13 (6) |
| **1825** | | | |
| 7 Feb. | Edward Jones, Bard to the King (second sale) | Sotheby | S.C.S. 140 (2) |
| 7 June | Dr Jameson, of Cheltenham | Musgrave | 7897.d.13 (8) |
| 30 March | Mr Sharpe, of Knutsford (in a mixed sale) | Musgrave | S.C. 1078 (10) |
| 30 June, 1 July | William Knyvett | Musgrave | C. 60.h.1 (17) |
| **1826** | | | |
| 13–15 Feb. | T. Jones, of Nottingham | — | Warren[1] |
| n.d. | Joseph Corfe[2] | — | — |
| **1827** | | | |
| 25 April | R. C. Sidney | Musgrave | 7897.d.13 (3) |
| **1828** | | | |
| 12 May | ⎰ John Sale ⎱ P. Taylor | Musgrave | Hirsch IV. 1087 |
| 10 July | ⎰ Joseph Gwilt ⎱ Giuseppe Naldi (residue) | Musgrave | 7897.d.13 (19) |
| **1829** | | | |
| 22 June | William Shield | Musgrave | 7897.d.13 (22) |
| **1830** | | | |
| 3–5 March | ⎰ Mathew Cooke ⎱ Benjamin Jacobs | Musgrave | (*Harmonicon*, 1830, pp. 136, 179) |
| **1832** | | | |
| 3 April | Thomas Greatorex (first sale) | Watson | C. 61.h.1 (21) |
| 26 June | John Sidney Hawkins (first sale) | Wheatley | S.C.W. 19 (4) |
| 26 June | Stephen Groombridge, Thomas Greatorex (second sale), John Sidney Hawkins (second sale: portion of music) | Watson | S.C. 1078 (2) |
| n.d. | Muzio Clementi | — | p. 91 |

[1] See p. 132, n. 2.    [2] Aylesford sale, 1873, lot 287.

| Date of sale | Name | Auctioneer, etc. | Location of sale-catalogue, or source of information |
|---|---|---|---|
| **1838** | | | |
| 17 Aug. | William Young Ottley | Sotheby | S.C.S. 220 (7) |
| 14 Dec. | William Kitchiner (second sale) | Sotheby | S.C.S. 221 (6) |
| **1839** | | | |
| 11 April | Samuel Prado (partly music in a mixed sale) | Evans | S.C.E. 60 (6) |
| **1841** | | | |
| 31 May | Joseph Warren (duplicates) | Fletcher | Harding[1] |
| **1842** | | | |
| 2 May | Rev. Ignatius Latrobe | Fletcher | Harding[1] |
| 27 May | Charles Britiffe Smith | Evans | Munby[2] |
| 5 July | James Hook | Fletcher | Harding[1] |
| **1843** | | | |
| 29 May | John Sidney Hawkins (third sale) | Evans | Harding[1] Munby[2] |
| 27 June | Thomas Vaughan | Fletcher | Harding[1] |
| 18 Dec. | J. D. Rohlff | Woodrow (Norwich) | *Musical World* (1843), p. 402, and *Norwich Mercury*, 18 Nov. 1843 |
| **1844** | | | |
| 24 April | John Stafford Smith | —[3] | p. 43 |
| | George Cooper | Fletcher | Harding[1] |
| 9 Dec. | Mrs Fawcett | | |
| | Ernest A. Kellner | | |
| **1845** | | | |
| 5 Feb. | Barham Livius | Fletcher | Harding[1] |
| 19 June | Miss Wainewright | Lewis | S.C.L. 16 (18) |
| 5, 6 Aug. | Benjamin Cooke | Fletcher | Harding[1] |
| **1846** | | | |
| 20 April | Augustus Frederick, Duke of Sussex | Christie | C. 61.h.1 (31) |
| 10 Aug. | Louis Gantter | Puttick | S.C.P. 1 (3) |
| **1847** | | | |
| 9 March | George Penson | Puttick | Harding[1] |
| 30 March | Johann Andreas Stumpff | Puttick | S.C.P. 2 (7) |
| 26 April | John Capel (lots 81–174 only comprise music) | Winstanley | C. 61.h.1 (34) |
| 22 May | Lady Mary Elizabeth Sykes | Puttick | S.C.P. 3 (5) |
| 14 June | Enoch Hawkins | Sotheby | S.C.S. 275 (4) |
| 23 July | {Ignaz Moscheles {An anonymous collection | Puttick | S.C.P. 3 (12) |
| 17 Dec. | [Henry John Gauntlett] | Puttick | S.C.P. 5 (1) |

[1] Private collection of Walter N. H. Harding, see p. 93.
[2] Private collection of A. N. L. Munby, King's College, Cambridge.
[3] 'an out of the way place in Gray's Inn Road.'

| Date of sale | Name | Auctioneer, etc. | Location of sale-catalogue, or source of information |
|---|---|---|---|
| **1848** | | | |
| 27 Jan. | Timothy Essex | Puttick | S.C.P. 5 (4) |
| 10 March | Rev. Samuel Picart | Puttick | S.C.P. 6 (1) |
| 12 April | Charles Hatchett | Puttick | S.C.P. 6 (7) |
| **1849** | | | |
| 23 March | Sir Giffin Wilson | Puttick | S.C.P. 9 (12) |
| 19, 20 April | C. Mathews | — | Warren[1] |
| 22 Dec. | Charles Chaulieu (first sale) | Puttick | S.C.P. 13 (5) |
| **1850** | | | |
| 19 June | John Scott | Sotheby | S.C.S. 325 (6) |
| 9 Aug. | Charles Chaulieu (second sale) | Puttick | S.C.P. 16 (6) |
| 28 Nov. | Adolphus Frederick, Duke of Cambridge | Puttick | S.C.P. 17 (3) |
| **1851** | | | |
| 14 Aug. | J. P. Street | Puttick | S.C.P. 21 (3) |
| 28 Aug. | Thomas Gray[2] (d. 1771) | Sotheby | S.C.S. 343 (4) |
| **1852** | | | |
| 25 June | Vincent Novello (first sale) | Puttick | S.C.P. 26 (4) |
| 27 Aug. | John Stafford Smith[3] | Puttick | S.C.P. 27 (6) |
| 12 Nov. | C. B. Tait (lots 1096–1120 only consist of music) | Tait & Nisbet | P.R. 2.C.5 (3) |
| **1853** | | | |
| 26 May | Thomas M. Alsager / George Henry Boscawen, 3rd Earl of Falmouth | Puttick | S.C.P. 31 (4) |
| 23 June | Richard Clark (first sale) | Puttick | S.C.P. 31 (7) |
| 25 June | George Butler, Dean of Peterborough / Richard Clark (second sale) / John Stokoe | Puttick | S.C.P. 32 (1) |
| 17 Aug. | John Stafford Smith[3] | Puttick | S.C.P. 32 (9) |
| **1854** | | | |
| 19 July | Signor Cerutti / T. Pymar / Clayton Freeling / Joseph Gwilt (second sale) | Puttick | S.C.P. 37 (2) |
| **1855** | | | |
| 30 April | Rev. James Baker / William Cramer | Puttick | S.C.P. 40 (6) |
| 14 June | Sir Henry Rowley Bishop (first sale) | Puttick | S.C.P. 41 (7) |
| **1856** | | | |
| 14 Oct. | George Gwilt | Puttick | S.C.P. 46 (8) |

[1] See p. 132, n. 2.     [2] Only lot 95 consists of music. See p. 49.
[3] A residue only, in the stock of Calkin & Budd.

| Date of sale | Name | Auctioneer, etc. | Location of sale-catalogue, or source of information |
|---|---|---|---|
| **1857** | | | |
| 2 May | Richard Clark (third sale) | Puttick | S.C.P. 49 (5) |
| 18 June | John Robinson | Puttick | S.C.P. 50 (3) |
| 28 Nov. | G. N. Jones | Puttick | S.C.P. 51 (11) |
| **1858** | | | |
| 3 July | William Ayrton | Puttick | S.C.P. 55 (2) |
| 2 Aug. | Rev. Richard Allott | Puttick | S.C.P. 55 (7) |
| **1859** | | | |
| 23 Feb. | Charles Danvers Hackett | Puttick | S.C.P. 57 (4) |
| 24 March | Ralph Willett | Puttick | S.C.P. 57 (7) |
| **1860** | | | |
| 12 Jan. | W. J. Brown | Puttick | S.C.P. 64 (3) |
| 10 Feb. | Adolphus Kent Oom | Puttick | S.C.P. 64 (7) |
| 24 April | Henry Forbes | Puttick | S.C.P. 66 (1) |
| 28 June | Sir Andrew Barnard / Sir George Smart | Puttick | S.C.P. 67 (4) |
| 20 Dec. | John Hullah (first sale) | Christie | C. 61.h.1 (85) |
| **1861** | | | |
| 21 Jan. | Thomas Taylor (lots 58–91 and 538–9, in a mixed sale)[1] | Sotheby | S.C.S. 492 (3) |
| 17 July | Frederick Perkins / Edward Rigby | Puttick | S.C.P. 76 (3) |
| **1862** | | | |
| 16 April | Charles Edward Horsley | Puttick | S.C.P. 80 (3) |
| 3 Sept. | Vincent Novello (second sale) | Puttick | S.C.P. 83 (7) |
| **1863** | | | |
| 4 March | Richard Randall / J. H. R. Chichester | Puttick | S.C.P. 86 (1) |
| 30 Nov. | Edward Taylor | Puttick | S.C.P. 90 (5) |
| **1864** | | | |
| 18 May | Thomas Attwood Walmisley | Puttick | S.C.P. 93 (4) |
| 2 July | William Hopwood | Puttick | S.C.P. 94 (5) |
| 4 July | Edward Hodges (a mixed sale) | Puttick | S.C.P. 94 (6) |
| **1865** | | | |
| 12 April | F.M.A. Venua (lots 369–565 only consist of music) | Puttick | S.C.P. 98 (9) |
| **1866** | | | |
| 12 July | Thomas Mackinlay | Puttick | S.C.P. 109 (6) |
| **1867** | | | |
| 20 Dec. | Edward Bates | Puttick | S.C.P. 119 (5) |
| **1869** | | | |
| 14–17 April | Samuel Arnold and J. T. Arnold (lots 1513–31 only consist of music) | Puttick | S.C.P. 128 (6) |
| 30 June | Charles Lucas | Puttick | S.C.P. 130 (3) |

[1] Lot 91 comprises 1500 Italian libretti of the eighteenth century, in manuscript.

| Date of sale | Name | Auctioneer, etc. | Location of sale-catalogue, or source of information |
|---|---|---|---|
| **1871** | | | |
| n.d. | Cipriani Potter | — | p. 92. |
| **1872** | | | |
| 23 Feb. | Joseph Warren (second sale) | Puttick | S.C.P. 146 (10) |
| 27 March | ⎧ Richard John Samuel<br>⎨ Stevens (d. 1837)<br>⎩ Thomas Kennedy | Puttick | S.C.P. 147 (6) |
| 23 May | Joseph Warren (third sale) | Puttick | S.C.P. 148 (7) |
| 28 June | Joseph Warren (fourth sale) | Puttick | S.C.P. 150 (8) |
| 15 Nov. | ⎰ George French Flowers<br>⎱ William Hawes | Puttick | S.C.P. 152 (9) |
| **1873** | | | |
| 20 Feb. | William Crotch (d. 1847,<br>  first sale) | Puttick | S.C.P. 154 (8) |
| 24 April | Thomas Oliphant | Puttick | S.C.P. 155 (8) |
| 30 June | John Shoubridge | Puttick | S.C.P. 156 (12) |
| 25 Aug. | Heneage Finch, 6th Earl of<br>  Aylesford (a mixed sale) | Puttick | S.C.P. 157 (14) |
| 30 Oct. | ⎧ J. L. Hopkins<br>⎨ Prince Stanislaw<br>⎩  Poniatowski | Puttick | S.C.P. 158 (2) |
| 1 Dec. | John Lodge Ellerton | Puttick | S.C.P. 158 (8) |
| **1874** | | | |
| 30 Jan. | James Hook (d. 1827)<br>  (a mixed sale) | Puttick | S.C.P. 160 (1) |
| 20 April | Thomas Moore (d. 1847)<br>  (lots 164–96 only consist of<br>  music) | Puttick | S.C.P. 161 (7) |
| **1875** | | | |
| 26 April | Sir William Sterndale Bennett<br>  (first sale) | Puttick | S.C.P. 167 (6) |
| 31 May | Maria Hackett (lots 1166–<br>  1408 in a mixed sale) | Puttick | S.C.P. 168 (3) |
| 26 July | Edward Chippindale | Puttick | S.C.P. 169 (5) |
| 16 Aug. | Sampson Moore (a mixed<br>  sale) | Puttick | S.C.P. 169 (10) |
| **1876** | | | |
| 31 July | Miss Elizabeth Masson | Puttick | S.C.P. 175 (6) |
| 24 Nov. | Alfred Angel | Puttick | S.C.P. 176 (12) |
| 18 Dec. | Thomas Pickering | Sotheby | S.C.S. 746 (5) |
| **1877** | | | |
| 30 Jan. | August Friedrich Christoph<br>  Kollmann (d. 1829) | Puttick | S.C.P. 177 (10) |
| 28 June | William Crotch (second sale) | Puttick | S.C.P. 180 (12) |
| 31 July–7 Aug. | Edward Francis Rimbault | Sotheby | S.C.S. 758 (2) |
| 22 Aug. | Edward J. Card | Puttick | S.C.P. 181 (13) |
| 27 Nov. | George Townshend Smith | Puttick | S.C.P. 182 (14) |

| Date of sale | Name | Auctioneer, etc. | Location of sale-catalogue, or source of information |
|---|---|---|---|
| **1878** | | | |
| 4 Feb. | Rev. Edward Goddard | Sotheby | S.C.S. 764 (3) |
| 28 March | Christopher Lonsdale | Sotheby | S.C.S. 767 (7) |
| 27 May | R. P. Carr | Sotheby | S.C.S. 771 (2) |
| 15 Oct. | {Sir William Sterndale Bennett (second sale) James King | Puttick | S.C.P. 187 (1) |
| **1879** | | | |
| 24 Feb. | William Williams | Puttick | S.C.P. 189 (4) |
| 30 June | William Snoxell | Puttick | S.C.P. 191 (11) |
| 15 Dec. | Frederick Smee | Puttick | S.C.P. 194 (2) |
| **1880** | | | |
| 19 Jan. | John Reekes | Puttick | S.C.P. 194 (11) |
| 22 March | {Dr Scholfield Thomas Carter | Puttick | S.C.P. 195 (14) |
| 19 April | Joseph Thomas Cooper | Puttick | S.C.P. 196 (1) |
| 20 Dec. | John Fitchett Marsh | Puttick | S.C.P. 200 (5) |
| **1881** | | | |
| 21 Feb. | Mrs Mapleson, senior (lots 215–384 in an anonymous sale) | Puttick | S.C.P. 201 (5) |
| 8 April | Joseph Warren (fifth sale) | Puttick | S.C.P. 201 (19) |
| 25 April | William Sharp | Puttick | S.C.P. 202 (4) |
| 22 June | J. F. Stanford | Puttick | S.C.P. 203 (1) |
| 7 July | {Carl Engel Joseph Warren (sixth sale) | Puttick | S.C.P. 203 (5) |
| 18 Oct. | James Coward | Puttick | S.C.P. 204 (3) |
| **1882** | | | |
| 23 Jan. | John Bianchi Taylor (lots 1–117 in a mixed sale) | Puttick | S.C.P. 206 (7) |
| 4 May | {Carl Engel (second sale) Charles Goodban | Puttick | S.C.P. 207 (1) |
| 23 June | John Barker Plumb | Puttick | S.C.P. 209 (1) |
| **1883** | | | |
| 27 May | John Blockley (lots 523–702 only consist of music) | Puttick | S.C.P. 213 (11) |
| 17 Aug. | William Laidlaw (first sale) | Puttick | S.C.P. 215 (9) |
| 22 Aug. | William Laidlaw (second sale) | Puttick | S.C.P. 215 (10) |
| 27 Nov. | Stephen Nicholson Barber | Puttick | S.C.P. 216 (12) |
| **1884** | | | |
| 25 June | John Hullah (second sale) | Puttick | S.C.P. 220 (5) |
| 26 June | Julian Marshall (first sale)[1] | Sotheby | S.C.S. 875 (5) |
| 29 July | Julian Marshall (second sale) | Sotheby | S.C.S. 878 (1) |
| 25 Nov | George Benson | Puttick | S.C.P. 221 (10) |

[1] Lots 1–127 only relate to music, comprising autograph letters of musicians. In the anonymous sale of Marshall's general library (25 April 1870, S.C.S. 630 (2)) lots 410–17 comprised part-books of early English music.

| Date of sale | Name | Auctioneer, etc. | Location of sale-catalogue, or source of information |
|---|---|---|---|
| **1885** | | | |
| 29 Jan. | Sir John Goss (first sale) | Puttick | S.C.P. 222 (10) |
| | Rev. Arthur Robert Ward | | |
| 8 April | Sir John Goss (second sale) | Puttick | S.C.P. 223 (10) |
| 6 July | J. Carnaby | Sotheby | S.C.S. 892 (3) |
| | J. Harvey | | |
| 24 Nov. | William Henry Stone (first sale) | Puttick | S.C.P. 226 (12) |
| | James Smyth | | |
| | Harold Thomas | | |
| **1886** | | | |
| 22 March | William Henry Stone (second sale) | Puttick | S.C.P. 227 (20) |
| | John Bernard Sale | | |
| 10 June | Josiah Pittman | Puttick | S.C.P. 229 (2) |
| 5 July | Robert S. Callcott | Puttick | S.C.P. 229 (10) |
| **1887** | | | |
| 22 Feb. | John Fane, Earl of Westmorland | Puttick | S.C.P. 231 (17) |
| 17 Aug. | Alfred Kew | Puttick | S.C.P. 235 (13) |
| 7 Nov. | William Henry Husk | Puttick | S.C.P. 236 (9) |
| | Thomas Hickson | | |
| **1888** | | | |
| 23 Jan. | Rev. Samuel Stephenson Greathed | Puttick | S.C.P. 237 (8) |
| | Sir Henry Rowley Bishop (second sale) | | |
| 14 March | James Henry Mapleson (first sale) | Puttick | S.C.P. 237 (21) |
| 28 May | James Henry Mapleson (second sale) | Puttick | S.C.P. 239 (1) |
| 27 July | C. J. Reed (a mixed sale) | Puttick | S.C.P. 240 (6) |
| **1889** | | | |
| 22 Nov. | John Dobson | Sotheby | S.C.S. 979 (4) |
| **1890** | | | |
| 17 Feb. | Alexander Foote (lots 1–119 in a mixed sale) | Sotheby | S.C.S. 984 (6) |
| **1895** | | | |
| 5 July | Andrew George Kurtz (lots 41–121, in a mixed sale, are of predominantly musical interest) | Sotheby | S.C.S. 1088 (7) |
| **1904** | | | |
| 11, 12 July | Julian Marshall (third sale)[1] | Sotheby | —[2] |

[1] About 90 lots only of music in his general library.
[2] No individual pressmarks are given for catalogues of sales held after 1900. See p. 131.

# Classified Lists of Past Collectors

| Date of sale | Name | Auctioneer, etc. | Location of sale-catalogue, or source of information |
|---|---|---|---|
| **1905** | | | |
| 3, 4 July | Thomas William Taphouse[1] | Sotheby | — |
| **1917** | | | |
| 17–24 May | William Hayman Cummings | Sotheby | — |
| **1918** | | | |
| 13 May | Charles Wightwick Finch, 8th Earl of Aylesford (lots 201–326c only consist of music, in a mixed sale) Alfred Henry Littleton (lots 1–200, in a mixed sale) | Sotheby | — |
| **1919** | | | |
| 15 Dec. | Sydney Richardson Christie-Miller | Sotheby | — |
| **1924** | | | |
| 2 July | Sir Frederick Bridge | Hodgson | — |
| **1925** | | | |
| 26 June | William Alexander Barrett (d. 1891) | Hodgson | — |
| **1934** | | | |
| 5 Dec. | Sir John Stainer (d. 1901) | Hodgson | — |
| **1935** | | | |
| 1–3 April | Miss Ellen Ann Willmott | Sotheby | — |
| **1939** | | | |
| 13, 14 Feb. | Godfrey Edward Pellew Arkwright (first sale) | Sotheby | — |
| **1940** | | | |
| 24, 25 June | Edward Speyer (first sale) | Sotheby | — |
| 2 July | Edward Speyer (second sale) (lots 489–503 only consisted of music) | Sotheby | — |
| **1944** | | | |
| 5 Dec. | Godfrey Edward Pellew Arkwright (second sale, residue) | Sotheby | — |
| **1945** | | | |
| 26 June | Arthur Henry Mann | Sotheby | — |
| **1947** | | | |
| 16, 17 June | Arthur Frederick Hill | Sotheby | — |
| **1952** | | | |
| 15–17 Dec. | Edward Henry William Meyerstein (lots 279–378 only consist of music) | Sotheby | — |

[1] 123 lots were purchased by Leeds Public Libraries.

| Date of sale | Name | Auctioneer, etc. | Location of sale-catalogue, or source of information |
|---|---|---|---|
| **1954** | | | |
| 11, 12 Oct. | William Westley Manning (148 lots of music and autograph letters, etc., of composers in a general collection) | Sotheby | — |
| **1958** | | | |
| 21 Jan. | Edward Joseph Dent (lots 312–458 in a mixed sale) John Brande Trend (lots 506–31 in a mixed sale) | Sotheby | — |
| **1959** | | | |
| 11, 12 May | Cecil Bernard Oldman (lots 205–69 in a mixed sale) | Sotheby | — |
| 10 Dec. | Ernest Newman | Hodgson | — |
| **1960** | | | |
| 19 Dec. | Harold Reeves (lots 137–210 in a mixed sale) | Sotheby | — |

## (b) UNNAMED COLLECTORS

| Date of sale | Description | Auctioneer | Sale-catalogue |
|---|---|---|---|
| **1813** | | | |
| 18 Feb. | Anon.[1] | White | S.C. 1076 (6) |
| 27 April | A professor | White | S.C. 1076 (3) |
| **1821** | | | |
| 12 Dec. | 'Several persons, deceased' | White | 7897.d.13 (3) |
| **1822** | | | |
| 15 May | A professor | Musgrave | S.C. 1078 (8) |
| 3 July | An amateur | Musgrave | S.C. 1078 (4) |
| **1823** | | | |
| 10 July | 'a library...to be disposed of under peculiar circumstances' | Musgrave | 7897.d.13 (4) |
| **1826** | | | |
| 1, 2 May | Anon. | Musgrave | 7897.d.13 (10) |
| 13 Dec. | Anon. | Musgrave | 7897.d.13 (11) |
| **1827** | | | |
| 7 March | Anon. | Musgrave | 7897.d.13 (12) |
| 14 Dec. | Anon. | Musgrave | 7897.d.13 (14) |
| **1828** | | | |
| 18 March | Anon. | Musgrave | 7897.d.13 (16) |
| **1829** | | | |
| 26 Sept. | Anon. | Musgrave | 7897.d.13 (25) |

[1] Used here to signify that the title-page does not give any description of the owner.

# Classified Lists of Past Collectors

| Date of sale | Description | Auctioneer | Sale-catalogue |
|---|---|---|---|
| **1841** | | | |
| 13 Sept. | A gentleman | Fletcher | Harding[1] |
| **1844** | | | |
| 29 April | Anon. | Fletcher | Harding[1] |
| **1845** | | | |
| 28 March | Two well-known amateurs | Fletcher | Harding[1] |
| **1847** | | | |
| 23 July | { Anon.<br>{ I. Moscheles | Puttick | S.C.P. 3 (12) |
| **1849** | | | |
| 19 Feb. | Anon. (stated in MS. note to be part of Warren's music) | Puttick | Harding[1] |
| 23 June | A distinguished professor | Puttick | Harding[1] |
| 31 August | Anon. | Puttick | Harding[1] |
| **1852** | | | |
| 8 Jan. | A professor, deceased | Puttick | S.C.P. 23 (3) |
| **1854** | | | |
| 4 Feb. | A distinguished professor, deceased | Puttick | S.C.P. 34 (5) |
| **1861** | | | |
| 10 June | A well-known collector | Puttick | S.C.P. 75 (3) |
| 6 Sept. | An amateur | Puttick | S.C.P. 77 (6) |
| **1862** | | | |
| 6 Jan. | A well-known collector | Puttick | S.C.P. 78 (9) |
| 20 Nov. | A professor | Puttick | S.C.P. 84 (2) |
| **1863** | | | |
| 29 April | An amateur | Puttick | S.C.P. 86 (9) |
| **1864** | | | |
| 22 Aug. | A professor | Puttick | S.C.P. 95 (6) |
| **1866** | | | |
| 2 March | Anon. | Puttick | S.C.P. 105 (7) |
| **1867** | | | |
| 11 Jan. | Several amateurs and professors | Puttick | S.C.P. 112 (6) |
| 21 Feb. | Anon. | Puttick | S.C.P. 113 (3) |
| 18 Nov. | Anon. | Puttick | S.C.P. 118 (5) |
| **1869** | | | |
| 24 April | [? Anon.: no title-page] | Puttick | S.C.P. 128 (7) |
| **1870** | | | |
| 25 June | Anon. | Puttick | S.C.P. 137 (4) |

[1] See p. 135, n. 1.

| Date of sale | Description | Auctioneer | Sale-catalogue |
|---|---|---|---|
| **1871** | | | |
| 28 July | A professor | Puttick | S.C.P. 144 (4) |
| 27 Nov. | A professor | Puttick | S.C.P. 145 (7) |
| **1872** | | | |
| 26 April | Anon. | Puttick | S.C.P. 148 (1) |
| 12 July | Anon. | Sotheby | S.C.S. 673 (1) |
| 28 Oct. | A professor | Puttick | S.C.P. 152 (3) |
| **1873** | | | |
| 29 April | A professor | Puttick | S.C.P. 155 (10) |
| **1874** | | | |
| 23 Feb. | Anon. | Sotheby | S.C.S. 698 (5) |
| 29 May | A musician, deceased | Puttick | S.C.P. 162 (6) |
| **1876** | | | |
| 29 May | A well-known professor | Puttick | S.C.P. 174 (3) |
| **1878** | | | |
| 27 Feb. | A gentleman | Puttick | S.C.P. 184 (1) |
| 24 June | A distinguished professor | Puttick | S.C.P. 186 (2) |
| **1879** | | | |
| 24 Jan. | Anon. | Puttick | S.C.P. 188 (13) |
| 24 March | A well-known professor | Puttick | S.C.P. 189 (13) |
| **1880** | | | |
| 24 May | A distinguished professor | Puttick | S.C.P. 196 (11) |
| **1881** | | | |
| 21 Feb. | { Anon.<br>Mrs Mapleson, senior,<br>  lots 215–384 | Puttick | S.C.P. 201 (5) |
| **1883** | | | |
| 17 July | Anon. | Sotheby | S.C.S. 858 (1) |
| **1884** | | | |
| 29 July | A well-known collector,<br>residing abroad | Puttick | S.C.P. 220 (15) |
| 11 Nov. | Anon. | Sotheby | S.C.S. 880 (4) |
| **1887** | | | |
| 25 May | A distinguished amateur | Puttick | S.C.P. 234 (5) |

# GROUP 2

## COLLECTORS WHOSE MUSIC HAS BEEN CONSERVED INTACT, IN WHOLE OR PART

*Abbreviations in second column:* b. = bequest; d. = donation; s. = sale

| Name | Method of conservation | Recipient and date of acquisition, if known |
|---|---|---|
| William Heather (d. 1627) | b. | University Music School, Oxford, 1627; deposited in the Bodleian Library, 1885 |
| Sir Edward Filmer (d. 1653: some additions by later generations) | s. | Yale University, 1946 |
| Thomas Hamond (d. 1662) | s. (?) | Ultimately acquired by the Rev. Osborne Wight and included in his music bequeathed to the Bodleian Library, 1801 |
| John Cosin, Bishop of Durham (d. 1672) | d. | Peterhouse, Cambridge, ?c. 1635 |
| Henry May (d. ?c. 1680) | d. | Pembroke College, Cambridge, ?1642/3[1] |
| Samuel Pepys (d. 1703) | b. | John Jackson, 1703 (life interest); then to Magdalene College, Cambridge, 1724 |
| Henry Aldrich (d. 1710) | b. | Christ Church, Oxford, 1710 |
| Narcissus Marsh, Archbishop of Dublin (d. 1713) | b. | Archbishop Marsh's Library, Dublin, 1713 |
| Richard Goodson (d. 1718) | b. | Christ Church, Oxford, 1718 |
| Philip Falle, Canon of Durham (d. 1742) | b. | Durham Cathedral Library, 1742 |
| Sir John Hawkins (d. 1789) | | |
| (i) Printed theoretical treatises | d. | British Museum, 1777 |
| (ii) Sixteenth- and seventeenth-century printed part-books | d. | King's Music Library, before 1785 |
| (iii) Various manuscripts | d. | British Museum, 1789 |
| Sir Henry Mackworth (d. 1791) | s. | R. Bonner Morgan, 1919; presented by him after purchase, to Cardiff Public Libraries |
| Cecil Brownlow, 9th Earl of Burghley (d. 1793) | – | 6th Marquis of Exeter (Burghley House, nr Stamford) |
| Rev. Osborne Wight (d. 1801) | b. | Bodleian Library, 1801 |
| General John Reid (d. 1806) | b. | Edinburgh University, 1806 |
| Richard Fitzwilliam, 7th Viscount Fitzwilliam (d. 1816) | b. | Fitzwilliam Museum, Cambridge, 1816 |
| Domenico Dragonetti (d. 1846) | b. | Mostly to the British Museum, 1846; partly given to Vincent Novello |
| John Wighton (d. 1866) | b. | Dundee Public Libraries, 1884 |
| William Euing (d. 1874) | b. | Anderson's College, Glasgow, 1874; transferred to Glasgow University, 1936 |

[1] May was ejected from the college in 1644, aged 21 (Venn).

# Some British Collectors of Music

| Name | Method of conservation | Recipient and date of acquisition, if known |
|---|---|---|
| Sir Frederick Ouseley, Bart. (d. 1889) | b. | St Michael's College, Tenbury, 1889 |
| Jasper Joly (d. 1892) | d. | National Library of Ireland, Dublin, 1863 |
| Andrew George Kurtz (d. 1895) (autograph letters of musicians) | b. | British Museum, 1895 |
| Venceslao Hugo Zavertal (d. 1899) | b. | Ladislao Zavertal, 1899; presented by him to University Library, Glasgow, 1934 |
| Richard Pendlebury (d. 1902) | d. & b. | Fitzwilliam Museum, Cambridge, 1882–1902; transferred to the Faculty of Music, 1925/6 |
| Julian Marshall (d. 1903) | | |
|    Handel scores and libretti | s. | Arthur James Balfour (later first Earl of Balfour), 1876; acquired after his decease by National Library of Scotland, Edinburgh, 1938 |
| John Glen (d. 1904) | s. | Lady Dorothea Ruggles-Brise, 1904; presented by her to the National Library of Scotland, Edinburgh, 1927 |
| Ebenezer Prout (d. 1909) | s. | Trinity College, Dublin, 1909 |
| William Lawrence Taylor (d. 1910) | b. | Aberdeen University, 1910 |
| Henry Watson (d. 1911) | d. | Manchester Public Library, 1902 |
| Rev. John Julian (d. 1913) | b. | Mostly to Church House, Westminster, 1913?; thence presented to the British Museum, 1949 |
| Cecil Sharp (d. 1924) | b. | English Folk Song & Dance Society (Cecil Sharp House, London, N.W. 1); manuscripts to Clare College, Cambridge, 1924 |
| Frank Kidson (d. 1926) | b. | Mitchell Library, Glasgow; a smaller portion to Leeds Public Libraries, 1926 |
| Louis Thompson Rowe (d. 1927) | b. | King's College, Cambridge, 1927 |
| Alexander Cowan (d. 1929) | b. | National Library of Scotland, Edinburgh, 1929 |
| Alexander Wood Inglis (d. 1929) | b. | National Library of Scotland, Edinburgh, 1929 |
| Arthur Henry Mann (d. 1929) | d.[1] | King's College, Cambridge, 1930 |
|   (i) Handeliana, eighteenth-century song-books, *etc.* | | |
|   (ii) English Hymnals and Psalms | | Church House, Westminster, 1930?; thence to the British Museum, 1949 |
|   (iii) Hook autographs | | University Library, Cambridge, 1929 |
|   (iv) Crotch collection | | Norwich Public Library, 1941 |
| J. A. Fuller-Maitland (d. 1936) Manuscripts of English Church Music | b. | Lancaster County Library; deposited on loan in Liverpool University Library |
| Charles Sanford Terry (d. 1936) | d. | By his widow to the Royal College of Music, London, 1936; on loan to the University Music School, Oxford |
| Franck Thomas Arnold (d. 1940) | b. | University Library, Cambridge, 1940 |
| Sir Donald Francis Tovey (d. 1940) | b. | Reid Music Library, Edinburgh University, 1940 |
| Ralph Griffin (d. 1942) | d. | Mostly to Fitzwilliam Museum, Cambridge, *c.* 1925 onwards |

[1] By members of Mann's family.

| Name | Method of conservation | Recipient and date of acquisition, if known |
|---|---|---|
| Edward Heron-Allen (d. 1943) | b. | Royal College of Music, London, 1943; on loan to the University Music School, Oxford |
| Paul Victor Mendelssohn Benecke (d. 1944) | b. | Margaret Deneke; deposited on loan in the Bodleian Library, c. 1950 onwards |
| Edwin Evans (d. 1945) | s. | Central Music Library, London, S.W. 1, 1947 |
| Gerald Melbourne Cooper (d. 1947) | b. | E. J. Dent, 1947; given by him mainly to Central Music Library, London, S.W. 1 |
| Arthur Henry Fox Strangways (d. 1948) | s. | British Broadcasting Corporation, 1945 |
| Thomas William Bourne (d. 1948) | b. | Bodleian Library, 1948 |
| Paul Hirsch (d. 1951) | s. | British Museum, 1946 |
| Edward Henry William Meyerstein (d. 1952) | b. | British Museum, 1952 |
| Marion Margaret Scott (d. 1955) | b. | University Library, Cambridge, 1955 |
| Gerald Finzi (d. 1956) | b. | Christopher Finzi, 1956 |
| Percy Scholes (d. 1958) | | |
|   (i) Burney collection | s. | James Osborn (Yale University) |
|   (ii) General collection | s. | National Library of Canada, Ottawa, 1957 |
| Rev. Maurice Frost (d. 1961) | b. | Part to the Royal School of Church Music, Addington, Surrey, 1961 |
| | | |
| Cecil Hopkinson | d. | National Library of Scotland, Edinburgh, 1952 |
| Henry George Farmer | d. | Glasgow University Library |
|   (i) Oriental music | | 1936 |
|   (ii) Old Scottish music | | 1950 |
|   (iii) Scottish composers of nineteenth and twentieth centuries | | 1941–50 |
| Cecil Bernard Oldman | d. | British Museum, 1960 onwards |

# GROUP 3

## COLLECTORS WHOSE MUSIC WAS DISPERSED

| Name | Period or medium of dispersal |
|---|---|
| Edward Paston (d. 1630) | ?Early seventeenth century |
| Sir Peter Leicester (d. 1678) | ?Early eighteenth century[1] |
| Sir Samuel Moreland (d. 1695) | Buried, 1695 |
| John Evelyn (d. 1706) | ?Early eighteenth century |
| James Bridges, first Duke of Chandos (d. 1744) | Late eighteenth century |
| Johann Christoph Pepusch (d. 1752) | Bequeathed, but without subsequent trace, to Ephraim Kelner, John Travers, and to the Academy of Ancient Music |

[1] A list of his music and instruments is given in *Sir Peter Leicester. Charges to the Grand Jury at Quarter Sessions*, ed. E. M. Halcrow (Manchester, 1953), pp. 151, 152.

| Name | Period or medium of dispersal |
|---|---|
| Robert, Lord Clive (d. 1774) | A. Rosenthal, catalogue 10, 1948 |
| Sir John Hawkins (d. 1789) | ?Partly destroyed by fire, before 1785 |
| Sir Watkin Williams-Wynn, Bart. (d. 1789) | Early twentieth century |
| Cornewall, family (including Miss — Cornewall, A. M. Cornewall, and Frances Elizabeth Cornewall, afterwards Viscountess Hereford, d. 1864) | ?Early nineteenth century |
| John Bishop, of Cheltenham (d. 1890) | ?Before 1890[1] |
| John Skelton Bumpus (d. 1913) | ?After 1920 |
| Adolph Schloesser (d. 1913) | ? |
| James E. Matthew (d. 192?) | Bought by Leo Liepmannssohn (Berlin) in 1907[2] and variously dispersed |
| Richard Northcott (d. 1931) | Variously dispersed. Part sold by Ifan Kyrle Fletcher, catalogue 190, 1959 |
| Alfred Moffat (d. 1950) | Sold by Otto Haas, catalogue 20, 1945 |
| Henry John Laufer (d. 1956) | Partly sold by Hermann Baron, in various catalogues |
| Cecil Bernard Oldman | Sold by Hermann Baron, catalogue 53, 1961 |

# GROUP 4

## COLLECTORS OF UNCERTAIN STATUS

Those marked with an asterisk are included on the basis of evidence of ownership derived from the indexes to the three volumes of Hughes-Hughes's catalogue and that to the manuscripts in the Royal College of Music.

Conyers D'Arcy, 7th Lord D'Arcy de Knayth and 4th Lord Conyers (d. 1653)
William Child (d. 1697)
Matthew Hutton[3] (d. 1711)
Humphrey Wanley (d. 1726)
William Raylton (d. 1757)
Thomas Chilcot (d. 1766)
James Kent (d. 1776)
Henry Hase (*fl.c.*1780)
*Gabriel Mathias (*fl.c.*1780)

*James Mathias (*fl.c.*1780)
*Hester Needler[4] (d. 1783)

John Keeble (d. 1786)
*William Flackton (d. 1793)
John Alcock, the elder (d. 1806)
Frederick Nicolay (d. 1809)
*Sarah Sophia Banks (d. 1818)
*Daniel Carnley (*fl.c.*1830)
*Thomas Cheeseman (*fl.c.*1830)
*Rev. James Pears (*fl.c.*1840)
*William Charlton Frampton (*fl.c.*1850)
John Frederick Campbell, 1st Earl of Cawdor (d. 1860)
*W. J. Westbrook (*fl.c.*1870)

[1] *Descriptive Catalogue of rare Musical Works in the Library of John Bishop*, Cheltenham, *c.* 1885 (Hirsch 425).

[2] For £2500: see *Musical Times* (1908), p. 19.

[3] See Pamela J. Willetts, 'Music from the Circle of Anthony Wood at Oxford', *The British Museum Quarterly*, vol. XXIV (1961), pp. 71–5.

[4] Widow of the violinist Henry Needler: see Hawkins, p. 807.

# LIST OF PRINCIPAL SOURCES

ARKWRIGHT, Godfrey Edward Pellew
*Catalogue of Music in the Library of Christ Church, Oxford.* London, 1915, 23.

BRITISH MUSEUM
*List of Catalogues of English Book Sales, 1676–1900, now in the British Museum* [begun by Harold Mattingley, continued by I. A. K. Burnett and completed by A. W. Pollard]. [London], 1915.

DEUTSCH, Otto Erich
Article 'Collections, private', in the fifth edition of Grove's *Dictionary* (1954). The first article of its kind in any musical dictionary. It consists of a list of British collectors, arranged chronologically, followed by the date of auction or by the name of the person or institution to whom the music passed, if conserved intact. The list is not however accurate in detail.

FELLOWES, Edmund Horace
*The Catalogue of Manuscripts in the Library of St Michael's College, Tenbury.* Paris, 1934.

FULLER-MAITLAND, John Alexander, and MANN, Arthur Henry
*Catalogue of the Music in the Fitzwilliam Museum, Cambridge.* London, 1893.

GROVE, Sir George (ed.)
*A Dictionary of Music and Musicians* (London, 1878–90). Issued in parts. Reissued in 4 vols. in 1890, with an appendix and a separate index.
—— Second edition, edited by J. A. Fuller-Maitland, 5 vols. (London, 1904–10).
Both editions contain many articles on British musicians who were also collectors.

HAWKINS, Sir John
*A General History of the Science and Practice of Music*, 4 vols. (London, 1776).
—— New edition, with the author's posthumous notes, 3 vols. (London, 1853).
Vol. III comprises portraits.
—— Reprinted, London, 1875.
In the present book reference is made to the 1853 edition.

HUGHES-HUGHES, Augustus
*Catalogue of Manuscript Music in the British Museum*, 3 vols. (London, 1906–9).

# Some British Collectors of Music

MADAN, Falconer [and others]

*A Summary Catalogue of Western Manuscripts in the Bodleian Library at Oxford*, 7 vols. (Oxford, 1895–1953).

The indexes comprising vol. VII include a general index of owners.

SQUIRE, William Barclay

Article 'Musical Libraries', in the first edition of Grove's *Dictionary*. Only the section on libraries in Great Britain and Ireland, including private collections, is Squire's work. He revised it for the second edition in which it was moved to the heading 'Libraries and Collections of Music'. In the third and fourth editions of the *Dictionary*, the article was revised by C. B. Oldman, and by Charles Cudworth in the fifth. All editions of the article give a good deal of information about the transmission of British private collections.

SQUIRE, William Barclay

*Catalogue of the Manuscripts in the Library of the Royal College of Music* [London, 1931].

Typescript. Contains a good deal of information about ownership. Copies are in the Students' Room of the Department of Manuscripts of the British Museum, and in the library of the Royal College of Music.

WAKELING, Donald Rufus

*English Auction Sales of Music and Literature of Music, 1691–1900. List of Catalogues* [1945].

Typescript. Mostly abstracted from the British Museum *List of Catalogues, etc.* Copies are in the Music Room of the British Museum and in the University Library, Cambridge.

WARREN, Joseph

[Autograph catalogue of his collection of music and musical literature. Begun 1849, maintained to *c.* 1870. In the possession of Cecil Hopkinson.]

# INDEX

*Figures followed by an asterisk refer to an auction-price paid for a musical work or other item.*

*Figures in bold type refer to the location of an auction sale-catalogue or to evidence that a sale took place.*

# Index

Augusta Sophia, Princess of Wales, 107, 120
  bookplate, 65
  owned *Amaryllis*, 107
  owned J. A. Hiller's *Die verwandelten Weiber*, 65
Augustus Frederick, Duke of Sussex, 51, 96
  collection described, 44; sold, 44, **135** (1846)
Ausonius, Decimus Magnus, quoted, 13
Autograph letters and documents of musicians,
    collected by
  Andrew George Kurtz, 68
  Thomas Mackinlay, 44
  William Westley Manning, 78
  Harold Reeves, 79
  Charles Britiffe Smith, 38
Avison, Charles, 17, 48, 80
Awbery, John, 24
Aylesford, Charles Wightwick Finch, 8th Earl of,
  *see* Finch
Aylesford, Heneage Finch, 6th Earl of, *see* Finch
Aylward, Theodore, 82
Ayrton, William, 70, 99
  bought a theorbo-lute by Maler, 46★
  collection described, 52, 53; sold, 52, **137** (1858)

Bach, Carl Philipp Emanuel, 26, 43, 76, 79
Bach, Cecilia, possible gift of Johann Christian
    Bach's autographs to Queen Charlotte,
    107 n.
Bach, Johann Christian, 107, 121, 122
  autographs in the Fitzwilliam Museum, 108 n.;
    in Royal Music Library, 108
  *Orione*, MS, 128
Bach, Johann Sebastian, 22, 26, 35, 43, 45, 48, 54,
    61, 74, 76, 83
  autograph music, 80
  grand studies for the organ with double-bass
    part by Dragonetti, 45
  MSS. in the Royal Music Library, 108
  Trios, 'believed to be autograph', 47
Bach, Wilhelm Friedrich Ernst, 17
Bach-Gesellschaft Edition, subscribed to by
    Queen Victoria, 113
Bach Society, 92 n.
Bacon, John, collection mentioned, 93
Baker, Charles Henry Collins, 16 n.
Baker, James, collection mentioned, 95; sold, **136**
  (1855)
Baker, Muriel Isabella, 16 n.
Baldwin, John, 105
Balfe, Michael William, 47
Balfour, Arthur James, 1st Earl Balfour, 79
Balham, London, 63
Balham, Mr —, collection sold, **132** (1802)
Baltzar, Thomas, MS. solos for violin, 26, 98★

Banister, John, and Low, Thomas, *Ayres and
    Dialogues*, 33★, 96★
Banks, Sarah Sophia, 148
Banner, Barbara, ix
Barber, Stephen Nicholson, collection sold, **139**
  (1883)
Barnard, Sir Andrew, collection sold, **137** (1860)
Baron, Hermann, ix
  collections sold
    Henry John Laufer, 76 n., 148
    Cecil Bernard Oldman, 79, 148
Barrett, Francis Ernest James Horace, 73
Barrett, William Alexander, collection described,
    73; sold, **141** (1925)
Barthélémon, François Hippolyte, collection men-
    tioned, 93; sold, **133** (1809)
Bartleman, John, 23, 31, 35, 56, 99, 101
  catalogue, unfinished, of Lord Fitzwilliam's
    music, 34
  collection described, 34, 35; sold, 34, **134** (1822)
Bassani, Giovanni Battista, 16
Bates, Edward, 96, 97, 99
  collection described, 56; sold, 56, **137** (1867)
Bates, Joah, 56
Bateson, Thomas, 40
Bath, 2 Gay Street, 91
*Bath Chronicle, The*, 91 n.
Bath Philharmonic Society, 26
Bathe, William, *Briefe Introduction to the Skill of
    Song*, 34
*Bay Psalm Book*, 100
Bedford, Francis, bookbindings done for Julian
    Marshall, 66
Beethoven, Ludwig van, 17, 28, 51, 79, 83, 111
  autograph letters, 38
  autograph music, 57, 61, 68, 76
  autograph in album owned by Sterndale Bennett,
    61
  nine autographs owned by Johann Andreas
    Stumpff, 46
  correspondence with Birchall, 63
  first and early editions, 74, 76
  hair in a locket, 46★
  satire on editions of, 62, 63
  Sonata op. 106, four leaves of autograph sketches,
    100★
  'Battle Symphony' performed at Windsor
    Castle, 58
  Pastoral Symphony, autograph sketches, 100★
  String trio, op. 3, engraver's MS., 66
  Archduke Trio, corrected proof sheets, 100★
  *Werke*, not subscribed to by Queen Victoria,
    113 n.; presented to Sir William Sterndale
    Bennett, 61

# Index

# Index

# Index

# Index

# Index

Handel Commemoration (1784), 25, 36, 56

Händel–Gesellschaft Edition, subscribed to by Queen Victoria, 113

Hanover, Court of, 105

Hardin, Elizabeth, *Six Lessons for the Harpsichord*, 127

Harding, Walter N. H., x, 42, 73, 92
  collection described, 82, 83
  sale-catalogues, formerly in Joseph Warren's collection, 93, 135, 136

Hardwicke Papers, 30

Harington, Henry, collection described, 26; sold, 26, **133** (1816)

Harley, Sir Robert, 1st Earl of Oxford, 7, 27

Harman, Richard Alexander, ix

*Harmonicon, The*, 27 n., 37 n., 52, 92, 134
  copy owned by the Duchess of Kent, 111

'Harmony', drawing by Michael Burghers, 52, 53 and n.★

Harp, by Erard, 47
  music for, 47

Harpsichord, owned by Lord Fitzwilliam, kept in Peterhouse, 36

Harpsichords, owned by Robert Orme, 12

Harris, James, 1st Earl of Malmesbury, 16

Harrison, Samuel, collection sold, 25, **133** (1814)

Harvard University Library, *see* Cambridge, Mass.

Harvey, J., collection sold, **140** (1885)

Hase, Henry, 148
  bookplate, and MSS. owned by, 91

Haslewood, John, 53

Haslewood, Joseph, 74

Hasse, Johann Adolph, *Ciro conosciuto*, MS., 128

Hatchett, Charles, collection sold, **136** (1848)

Hatton, John Liptrot, accompaniment to Paganini's caprices, 47

Hautbois, owned by Robert Orme, 12

Havergal, Henry, 43

Hawes, William, collection sold, **138** (1872)

Hawkins, Enoch, collection sold, 45, **135** (1847)

Hawkins, Sir John, 31, 90, 116 and n.
  acquainted with John Bartleman, 34
  as possible adviser to George III on buying old music, 126, 127
  as collector, 23
  collection described, 32, 33
  friendship with Boyce, 33
  *General History of the Science and Practice of Music*, 11, 15 and n., 94, 132, 148 n., 149; presented to George III, 122 and n.
  library burnt (1785), 110, 148
  library, gifts from
    madrigals, etc., to George III, 33, 110 and n.
    printed treatises, to British Museum, 145
    various MSS., to British Museum, 145

Hawkins, John Sidney, 45, 96
  collection described, 33; sold, 33, **134** (1832), 135 (1843)

Hawkins, Laetitia Matilda, 122 and n., 127

Hawksdon, Suffolk, 10

Haydn, Franz Joseph, 17, 22, 42, 45, 54, 79
  autographs, 38★, 76
  *Arianna in Naxos*, autograph, 63
  *Armida*, autograph, 48, 99★
  march in E flat, autograph, 58
  Missa S. Johannis, MS. score, corrected by the composer, 66
  'Teseo mio ben', autograph, 57

Hayes, Philip, 47, 110, 128 n.

Hayes, William, *Cathedral Music*, 127

Hayes, Philip and William, 24, 31, 56
  collection described, 21, 22; sold, 21, 132 (*c.* 1798)

Hayes, Richard James, ix

Hayward, John Davy, viii

Heather, William, 12, 23, 31, 68, 101
  collection and bindings described, 8
  collection bequeathed to the Music School, University of Oxford, 8, 145
  instruments mentioned, 8

Heber, Richard, 45, 51, 90

Hedley, Arthur, collection described, 80, 81

Heffer, Messrs W. and Sons, 88

Heirs of Stefan Zweig, 101
  collection described, 80

Helton, *see* Hilton, John

Henry Watson Library, Manchester, *see* Manchester, Public Libraries

Her Majesty's Theatre, London, 66

Herodotus, 20

Heron-Allen, Edith, 86

Heron-Allen, Edward
  bookplates, 86
  collection described, 86; bequeathed to the Royal College of Music, 86, 147

Heron-Allen, Marianna, 86

Hesse, Landgrave of, 23

Hickson, Thomas, collection sold, **140** (1887)

Highbury Place, London, 17

Hill, Arthur Frederick, collection described, 75; sold, **141** (1947)

Hilton, John, 40

Hinckley, Henry, collection described, 27; sold, 27, **134** (1822)

Hindle, John, 22

Hirsch, Olga, 63

Hirsch, Paul, 2
  collection described, 75; purchased by the British Museum, 75, 147

162

# Index

Liszt, Franz, 74, 79
  autograph letters, 79, 88
Littleton, Arthur Henry, 95
  collection described, 72; sold, **141** (1918)
Liverpool Philharmonic Society, 68
Liverpool University Library, collection of John
  Alexander Fuller–Maitland transferred to, 76
Livius, Barham, collection mentioned, 93; sold,
  **135** (1845)
Locke, Matthew, fantasias, 23
Lodwick, 47
Löhlein, Georg Simon, 81
London
  Clerkenwell, Mr Ward's House in Red Bull-
    Yard, 11, 131 n.
  Gray's Inn Road, 135 n.
  Henrietta St, the new house next the Wheat-
    sheaf, 12, 131 n.
  Highbury Place, 17
  Leadenhall Street, Musical Society at the Nag's
    Head (1770–8), 35
  Shoe Lane, 17
  Silver St, near Pulteney St, 132 n.
*London Spring Annual, The*, 112
London University, purchased books of musical
  theory from collection of Alfred Henry
  Littleton, 72
Longman, —, 35
Lonsdale, Christopher, 49, 92
  collection described, 63; sold, **139** (1878)
Lonsdale, R., 62
'Loosemore's five Bell Concert', 19
'Lord Oxford's Collection', *see* Harley, Sir Robert,
  1st Earl of Oxford
Lord's Cricket Ground, London, 94
Lorenzini, 39
Lucas, Charles, collection sold, **137** (1869)
Lully, Jean Baptiste, 36, 52, 74, 113
  operas, 20
Lumley, John, Lord, 7, 90
Lutes, owned by Robert Orme, 12
Lyskamm, the, Sir John Hawkins compared to, 33

McClean, Hugh, x
MacCunn, Hamish, 88
Mace, Thomas, 52, 89
McEwen, Sir John Blackwood, 88
Machaut, Guillaume de, 11
Mackeson, Charles, 16 n.
Mackinlay, Thomas, 79
  collection mentioned, 44; sold, 44, **137** (1866)
Mackworth, Sir Henry, collection described, 89;
  purchased for Cardiff Public Libraries by
  R. Bonner Morgan, 89, 145

Mackworth, Juliana, 89
Mackworth, Robert, 89
Mackworth-Young, Robert Christopher, viii
Madan, Falconer, *A Summary Catalogue of Western
  Manuscripts in the Bodleian Library at Oxford*,
  viii, 24 n., 149
Madden, Sir Frederic, 92 n.
Madrid, archives in, 119
Madrigal Society, the, 49, 59
Magdalene College, Cambridge, *see* Cambridge
  University
Maidstone, Kent, 89
Mainzer, Joseph, *Gaelic Psalm Tunes*, bound in
  tartan silk, 48
Malchair, John Baptist
  collection sold, 25 and n., **133** (1814)
  MS. Catalogue of the Aldrich and Goodson
    collections, 14 and n.
Maler, Laux, theorbo-lute by, in collections of
  Duke of Chandos and Ignaz Moscheles, 46
Malmesbury, James Harris, 1st Earl of, *see* Harris
*Manchester Public Free Libraries Quarterly Record*,
  85 n.
Manchester Public Libraries
  Henry Watson collection, gift of the, 85, 146
Manfrocce, Nicola Antonio, 28
Mann, Arthur Henry, 60
  collection described, 84; variously distributed,
    84, 146
  remainder of collection sold, **141** (1945)
  *see also* Fuller-Maitland, John Alexander, and
    Mann, A. H.
Manning, William Westley, collection described,
  78; sold, **142** (1954)
Mapleson, Mrs, senior, collection sold, 67 n., **139**
  (1881)
Mapleson, John Henry, collection described, 66,
  67; sold, **140** (1888)
Marenzio, Luca, 40
  Madrigals, 30★, 49★
Maria, Duchess of Gloucester, MS. music once
  owned by, now lost, 111
Marot, Clément, and Bèze, Théodore de, *Pseaumes
  de David*, 51
Marpurg, Friedrich Wilhelm, 52
Marsh, John Fitchett, collection described, 64; sold,
  **139** (1880)
Marsh, Narcissus, Archbishop of Cashel, etc.
  collection described, 15
  'Essay touching the (esteemed) sympathy be
    tween Lute or Viol Strings', 15
  music in the library founded by his bequest, 15, 145
  practice of music, 14
Marshall, Florence, 65

# Index

Marshall, Julian, 35, 56, 79, 98, 100, 113
  collection described, 64–6; sold, **139** (1884), **140** (1904)
  explanatory note in his autograph, xvi, pl. VIII
  sale of Handel items to Earl of Balfour, 146
Martin, Sir Theodore, 112 n.
Mary, Queen of England, 47
Mason, W., 100
Masson, Elizabeth, collection sold, **138** (1876)
Mathews, C., collection sold, **136** (1849)
Mathias, Gabriel, 148
Mathias, James, 148
Matterhorn, the, Charles Burney compared to, 31, 34
Matthew, James E., 90
  collection described, 71 and n.; dispersed by Leo Liepmannsohn, 148
  price paid for his collection, 148 n.
  typescript catalogue compiled by him, 71
May, Henry, assembled music for Pembroke College, Cambridge (c. 1642/3), 9 n., 145
Mee, John Henry, 23 n., 25 n.
Melton, see Milton, John
Mendelssohn, Paul Benecke, collection described, 86, 87; deposited in the Bodleian, 86, 147
Mendelssohn–Bartholdy, Jacob Ludwig Felix, 45, 47, 74, 86, 87
  *Athalia*, MS. score presented to Queen Victoria, 113
  autograph letters, 79
  autograph letters to Charles Coventry, 100
  autograph music, 76
  gift of J. S. Bach's music to C. E. Horsley, 54
  *Elijah*, 1st violin part MS. corrected by the composer, 100*
  'Hebrides' overture, autograph, 61*, 100*
  *Oedipus at Colonus*, MS. score presented to Queen Victoria, 113; performed at Buckingham Palace, 113
  *Six Organ Concertos*, proof copy, corrected by the composer, 50*
Mercadente, Saverio, 111
Messaeus, MSS. in the hand of, 15, 16
Meyer, Charles, bookbinder to Queen Charlotte, 123 n.
Meyerbeer, Giacomo, 54
  *Il Crociato*, composer's annotated copy, 52
  *Robert le Diable*, adapted by Sir Henry Bishop, 52
Meyerstein, Edward Henry William, 84
  collection described, 76; partly bequeathed to the British Museum, 76, 147; sold, **141** (1952)
Miller, Philip L., x
Milton, John, 40
Mischabel, the, Edward Jones compared to, 34

Mitchell Library, see Glasgow Public Libraries
Moccas Court, Herefordshire, 17
Moffat, Alfred, collection described, 78; dispersed, 148
Mondonville, Jean Joseph, 19
Monkhouse, Rev. Dr, collection described, 27, 28; sold, 27, **134** (1823)
Montagu, John, 4th Earl of Sandwich, 37
Monte Rosa, Lord Fitzwilliam compared to, 34
*Monthly Musical Record, The*, 108 n., 118 n.
Moore, Sampson, collection sold, **138** (1875)
Moore, Thomas
  collection sold, **138** (1874)
  owned a Paris edition of Mozart, 61
  song dedicated to the Duchess of Kent, 111
Moreland, Sir Samuel, collection described, 10, 147
Morelli, Cesare, 11
Morgan, R. Bonner, purchased the Mackworth Collection for Cardiff Public Library, 89, 145
Morley, Thomas, 40, 54
  *Canzonets*, 74*, 96*
  *Consort Lessons*, 35*, 49
  *First Book of Balletts*, 90 n.
  *Madrigals*, 96*
  *Plaine and easie Introduction*, 35*, 49, 94*, 95*, 127; annotated copy owned by Thomas Tomkins, 84
Morrell, W. T. & Co., bookbindings for Edward Heron-Allen, 86
Moscheles, Ignaz
  collection, mixed with 'other properties', 6; sold, 46, **135** (1847)
  owned a theorbo-lute by Laux Maler, 46
Mozart, afterwards Nissen, Constanze, 46
Mozart, Leopold
  earliest works of Wolfgang Mozart, in his hand, 76, 99*, 100*
  MS. violin part in his hand to Wolfgang Mozart's Sonatas (K. 10–15), 108
  *Reiseaufzeichnungen*, 121 and n.
Mozart, Wolfgang Amadeus, 17, 28, 32, 54, 61, 74, 112, 122
  Attwood's exercises supervised, with autograph additions, 73*, 99*
  autograph music, 57, 61, 76, 80
  autographs in the collection of Johann Andreas Stumpff, 99*
  autographs of particular works
    'La bergère Celimène', variations on, 68*, 99*
    Clarinet Trio (K. 498), 52, 99*
    'Das Veilchen', 80, 99*
    Duet-Sonatas (K. 497, K. 521), 83
    Fugue in C minor (K. 426), 99*

# Index

Mozart (*cont.*)
    Rondo in A minor (K. 511), 68★, 99★
    String Quintet in D (K. 593), 63, 99★
    'Verzeichnis aller meiner Werke', 80
    earliest works, in Leopold Mozart's hand, 76, 96★, 100★
    hair, 46
    printed works
        early editions, and literature about, 79
        *Gesamtausgabe*, 97★
        Sonatas (K. 10–15), offered to Queen Charlotte, 108
    relics, 88
Mozart Bicentenary Exhibition, British Museum (1956), 80
Mudge, eighteenth-century English composer, 80
Muffat, Gottlieb, *Componimenti musicali*, copy dedicated to Charles IV, 65
Muir, Percy, x
Mulliner Book, xv, 43★, 62, 97★, pl. VII
Multiple copies of music, sales of, 3
Munby, Alan Noel Latimer, x, 38 n., 135 n.
    *Cult of the Autograph Letter*, 38 n.
    *Phillipps Studies*, 45 n.
    sale-catalogues owned by, 135 and n.
Murray, Charles Fairfax
    owned MS. music formerly belonging to the Duchess of Gloucester, 111
    presented J. C. Bach MSS. to the Fitzwilliam Museum, 108
Musgrave, auctioneer
    sales of named collections
        William Boyce, the younger (1824), 28, **134**
        Mathew Cooke (1830), 92, **134**
        John Gunn (1824), 28, **134**
        Henry Hinckley (1822), **134**
        Benjamin Jacobs (1830), 92, **134**
        Dr Jameson (1825), 28, **134**
        William Knyvett (1825), 28, **134**
        Rev. Dr Monkhouse (1823), 27, **134**
        John Sale and P. Taylor (1828), 29, **134**
        Mr Sharpe (1825), 28, **134**
        R. C. Sidney (1827), 28, **134**
        William Shield (1829), 29, **134**
    sales of unnamed collections (1822, 1823, 1826–9), **142**
*Music & Letters*, 84 n., 87 n.
Music-collecting, beginnings of, 7
Music-collector, attempted definition of a, 7
*Musica Disciplina*, 9 n.
Musical Antiquarian Society, the, 95
*Musical Antiquary, The*, 74
Musical club at Oxford (*c.* 1675), 53
*Musical Library, The*, 52

'Musical Society at the Nag's Head, Leadenhall Street, 1770–8', 35
Musical Society of London, the, 55
*Musical Times, The*, 71 n., 148 n.
*Musical World, The*, 39–42, 135
'Musico-cartographers', 6
Myslivecek, Josef, 17

Naldi, Giuseppe, collection sold, 27, 28, **133** (1821), **134** (1828)
Napoleon, Emperor, 51
National Library of Canada, *see* Ottawa
National Library of Ireland, *see* Dublin
National Library of Scotland, *see* Edinburgh
Needler, Henry, 148 n.
Needler, Hester, 148
Neighbour, Oliver Wray, vii
New College, Oxford, *see* Oxford University
New York Public Library, Drexel MS. 4322, 62 n.
Nichols, John, 16
Nicolai, composers so named, 117
Nicolai, Valentino, 117
'Nicolay', 20 and n.
Nicolay, Augusta Georgiana, 120 n.
Nicolay, Bernard Underwood, 119, 121 n.
Nicolay, Christian Frederick, 119
Nicolay, Frederick, 25, 65 n., 148
    autograph index to a volume of Queen Charlotte's music, xv, pl. VI
    autograph list of lacunae in the autograph of Handel's *Deborah*, xv, pl. V
    autograph will, xv, 118, pl. IV
    bookplate described, 128
    as collector, 127
    owned twenty-three volumes of Handel's oratorios, 127, 128
Nicolay, Gaspard, 120
Nicolay, George, 121
Nicolay, Sapphira, 120
Nicolay, Sir William, 119, 127
Nicolay Papers, 120 n., 123
Nightingale, Florence, collection of opera libretti, 78
Nixon, Howard Millar, xi, 42 n.
Noblemen and Gentlemen's Catch Club, 20
Noland, Mr, 16
Norris, Thomas, 99
Northcott, Richard
    collection described, 80
    residue of collection sold, **148**
Norwich, City, 55
    Public Libraries, 84 n.
    received as gift part of the collection of Arthur Henry Mann, 84, 146

# Index

# Index

Puttick and Simpson (cont.)
 Joseph Gwilt (1854), **136**
 Charles Danvers Hackett (1859), **137**
 Maria Hackett (1875), **138**
 Charles Hatchett (1848), **136**
 William Hawes (1872), **138**
 Thomas Hickson (1887), **140**
 Edward Hodges (1864), **137**
 James Hook (1842), **135**; (1874), 59, 60, **138**
 J. L. Hopkins (1873), **138**
 William Hopwood (1864), **137**
 Charles Edward Horsley (1862), 55, **137**
 John Hullah (1884), 54, **139**
 William Henry Husk (1887), 66, **140**
 G. N. Jones (1857), **137**
 Thomas Kennedy (1872), **138**
 Alfred Kew (1887), **140**
 James King (1878), **139**
 August Friedrich Christoph Kollmann (1877), 60, **138**
 William Laidlaw (1883), 64, **139**
 Charles Lucas (1869), **137**
 Thomas Mackinlay (1866), **137**
 Mrs Mapleson (1881), **139**
 James Henry Mapleson (1888), **140**
 John Fitchett Marsh (1880), 64, **139**
 Elizabeth Masson (1876), **138**
 Sampson Moore (1875), **138**
 Thomas Moore (1874), **138**
 Ignaz Moscheles (1847), 46, **135**
 Vincent Novello (1852), 49, **136**; (1862), 49, 137
 Thomas Oliphant (1873), 59, **138**
 Adolphus Kent Oom (1860), **137**
 George Penson (1847), **135**
 Frederick Perkins (1861), **137**
 Samuel Picart (1848), 47, **136**
 Josiah Pittman (1886), **140**
 John Barker Plumb (1882), **139**
 Prince Stanislaw Poniatowski (1873), **138**
 T. Pymar (1854), **136**
 Richard Randall (1863), **137**
 C. J. Reed (1888), **140**
 John Reekes (1880), **139**
 Edward Rigby (1861), **137**
 John Robinson (1857), **137**
 John Bernard Sale (1886), **140**
 Dr Scholfield (1880), **139**
 William Sharp (1881), **139**
 John Shoubridge (1873), 59, **138**
 Sir George Smart (1860), 53, 54, **137**
 Frederick Smee (1879), 63, 64, **139**
 George Townshend Smith (1877), 63, **138**
 John Stafford Smith (residue: 1852, 1853), **136**
 James Smyth (1885), **140**
 William Snoxell (1879), **139**
 J. F. Stanford (1881), **139**
 Richard John Samuel Stevens (1872), 58, **138**
 William Henry Stone (1885, 1886), **140**
 J. P. Street (1851), **136**
 Johann Andreas Stumpff (1847), 46, **135**
 Lady Mary Elizabeth Sykes (1847), 45, **135**
 Edward Taylor (1863), 55, **137**
 John Bianchi Taylor (1882), **139**
 Harold Thomas (1885), **140**
 F. M. A. Venua (1865), **137**
 Arthur Robert Ward (1885), **140**
 Thomas Attwood Walmisley (1864), **137**
 Joseph Warren (1872), 56, 57, **138**; (1881), **139**
 Ralph Willett (1859), 137
 William Williams (1879), **139**
 Sir Giffin Wilson (1849), 47, **136**
 sales of unnamed collections
  (1847, 1849, 1852, 1854, 1861-4, 1866, 1867, 1869, 1870), **143**, (1871-4, 1876, 1878-81, 1884, 1887), **144**
Puttick, James Fell, 44
Pygott, Richard, 40
Pymar, T., collection sold, **136** (1854)
Pynson, Richard, printer of a fictitious edition of the *xx sōges* of 1530, 40, 41

Quaritch, Bernard, 97
Queen's Band, the, 122 n.
Queen's Band of Musick, the, 121
Queen's Chamber Band, the, 121, 128

*R.M.A. Research Chronicle*, 131 n.
Rameau, Jean Philippe, 36
Ramsden, Charles, 123 n.
Randall, Richard, collection sold, 56, 137 (1863)
Rastall, John, *The Four Elements*, 40
Rauzzini, Vincenzo, collection sold, 28, 91, **133** (1809, 1811)
Ravenscroft, John, *Sonate à tre*, 64
Ravenscroft, Thomas, the composer
 not a collector, 13
 *Briefe Discourse*, 40
 *Deuteromelia*, 40
 *Melismata*, 40
 *Musalia*, 1613 (a fictitious work), 40, 41
 *Pammelia*, 40
Ravenscroft, Thomas, Esq., a collector of books, 13
Ravenscroft, W., 13 n.
Rawlinson, Richard, 13 n.
Raylton, William, gave some music to William Gostling, 18
Read, —, music-dealer, 21
'Recitativas from ye opera at Venice 1646', 10

171

# Index

# Index

# Index